THE FATE OF YOUNG DEMOCRACIES

The recent backlash against democracy in such countries as Bolivia, Venezuela, Russia, and Georgia poses renewed concerns about the viability of this regime type in the developing world. Drawing on a data set of every democratization episode since 1960, this book explores the underlying reasons for backsliding and reversal in the world's fledgling democracies and offers some proposals with respect to what the international community might do to help these states stay on track toward political stability. Revising earlier scholarship on this topic, which focused on poor economic performance as the leading cause of democratic reversal, Ethan B. Kapstein and Nathan Converse argue that the core of the problem is found in the weak institutions that have been built in much of the developing world that allow leaders to abuse their power. Understanding the underlying reasons for democratic failure is essential if we are to offer policy recommendations that have any hope of making a difference on the ground.

Ethan B. Kapstein is Paul Dubrule Professor of Sustainable Development at INSEAD and a Visiting Fellow at the Center for Global Development in Washington, DC. He has also held academic appointments at the University of Minnesota and Harvard and served as an officer in the U.S. Navy, an international banker, and a Principal Administrator at the Organisation for Economic Co-operation and Development. He is the author or editor of ten books and numerous professional and policy articles in the field of international political economy. He is a member of the Council on Foreign Relations and the International Institute for Strategic Studies. Kapstein has received awards from the Rockefeller, Russell Sage, and Smith Richardson Foundations, and he has served as a consultant to many organizations in the public and private sectors.

Nathan Converse is a Ph.D. candidate in economics at the London School of Economics. Previously he was a research assistant at the Center for Global Development and at the International Institute of Finance.

The Fate of Young Democracies

Ethan B. Kapstein

INSEAD and Center for Global Development

Nathan Converse

London School of Economics

CAMBRIDGE UNIVERSITY PRESS
Cambridge, New York, Melbourne, Madrid, Cape Town, Singapore, São Paulo, Delhi

Cambridge University Press
32 Avenue of the Americas, New York, NY 10013-2473, USA

www.cambridge.org
Information on this title: www.cambridge.org/9780521732628

First published 2008

Printed in the United States of America

A catalog record for this publication is available from the British Library.

Library of Congress Cataloging in Publication Data

Kapstein, Ethan B.
The fate of young democracies / Ethan B. Kapstein, Nathan Converse.
    p. cm.
Includes bibliographical references and index.
ISBN 978-0-521-49423-6 (hardback)
1. Democracy – Developing countries.   2. Democratization – Developing countries.
I. Converse, Nathan, 1979–   II. Title.
JF60.K364   2009
321.809172′4–dc22   2008019072

ISBN   978-0-521-49423-6 hardback
ISBN   978-0-521-73262-8 paperback

This book is dedicated to Samuel P. Huntington

Contents

List of Figures and Tables

Figures

Preface and Acknowledgments

Sunny optimism about the durability and inevitable advance of democratization seems utterly misplaced.

Charles Tilly (2003)

The international community has good reason to be concerned by the fate of the world's young democracies (Freedom House, "Freedom in the World 2008," Press Release, January 16, 2008).[1] From Latin America to East Asia, constitutional arrangements and democratic institutions are under fire. Is the "third wave" of democratization (Huntington 1991) now receding? If so, what is causing the retreat?

Reports from the field indicate that democracy's health is fragile. During the research and writing of this book, for example, the democratically elected regime of Thanksin Shinwatra in Thailand was overthrown by a military coup in September 2006 (representing the *fourth* time that democracy had collapsed there), only to see a new but uneasy round of parliamentary elections held 16 months later. Meanwhile, a new move toward democratization in Pakistan (that country's *fifth*

---

[1] We use the terms *young democracies, young democratizers*, and *democratizers* interchangeably in this volume and our definitions (based on Polity IV rankings of regime type), methodology, and list of cases appear as Appendix 1. We use the term *democratic reversal* to refer to the overthrow of democracy (defined as a fall in the Polity score of 6 points or more) or what other authors have called *breakdown* (e.g., Bernhard et al. 2001, 2003; Gasiorowski and Power 1998).

attempt to establish this regime type) was marred by election-related violence culminating in the assassination of former Prime Minister Benazir
Bhutto. In Africa, elections in Kenya in late December 2007 that were
widely viewed as fraudulent led to widespread bloodletting along ethnic
lines.

Elsewhere, democracy in Fiji (the *second* episode of democracy in
that country) abruptly ended in a coup d'etat in December 2006, while in
January 2007 the military in Bangladesh conducted what might be called
a "soft" coup, maintaining the government in power while demanding
that it declare martial law in the face of a deteriorating political situation.
Recent power grabs by the leaders of such countries as Russia, Georgia, Venezuela, and Bolivia have all set back the cause of democracy in
those nations (Fish 2001; Freedom House, "Russia Downgraded to 'Not
Free,'" Press Release, December 20, 2004; Freedom House, "Freedom in
the Former Soviet Union Deteriorated in 2007," Press Release, January
23, 2008). Overall, at least half of the world's most recent democracies –
often referred to in the academic literature as being "unconsolidated,"
"fragile," or "partial" – are struggling to consolidate their institutions,
whereas several others have already reverted back to authoritarian rule
(Epstein et al. 2006).

Among the world's young and fragile democratizing states, we also
find a number of countries that have become vital to U.S. national security interests, including Afghanistan, Iraq, and, as already mentioned,
Pakistan in Southwest Asia. In the Middle East, Lebanon has struggled
for decades to build a stable democracy, while the government of any
newly established Palestinian state would surely face massive economic,
political, and social challenges. Ensuring that these young democracies
survive, consolidate, and prosper is therefore critical both to the leaders of those nations and to the foreign governments that support their
cause.

The purpose of this book is to contribute to the renewed academic
and public policy debates over the role of democracy in promoting long-
run political stability and economic growth, with a specific focus on the

differences between those young democracies that manage to consolidate their regimes and those that backslide or revert to authoritarianism. Simply stated, we argue that young democracies must put into place institutions and policies that disperse political and economic power if they are to survive. We further provide evidence that the problem of consolidating young democracies is particularly acute in deeply divided societies where structural or "initial conditions" like poverty, high concentrations of mineral wealth, or ethnic fragmentation may motivate politicians to centralize political and economic power rather than to distribute it more widely. Our analysis therefore leads us to adopt something like a classically pluralist vision of democratic governance.

We wish to stress, however, that we are *not* initial conditions "determinists." In fact, the data and case studies we present demonstrate that history is not always destiny. Even when leaders face severe structural constraints, they retain some room to maneuver, meaning that the institutional and policy choices they make and the *type* of democracy they establish matter greatly to their chances of forging durable regimes. Gideon Rose put it well when he wrote "it is precisely where circumstances leave off that the local democratizers' freedom of action begins" (Rose 2000/2001, 202).

The point is that political agency – the choices that actors make – is hardly irrelevant to a country's well-being. After all, if people truly had no agency, why would we study politics in the first place? In adopting this perspective we echo the words of Wilkie Collins, who wrote of his novel *The Moonstone*, "In some of my former novels the object proposed has been to trace the influence of circumstances upon character... the attempt made here is to trace the influence of character upon circumstances" (Collins 1868/1998).

Using the drier words of political economy, we argue that democracy builders serve their countries particularly well when they establish institutions that place effective constraints on executive authority. These constraints are of particular importance in divided or highly fragmented societies (including where elites are fragmented, as in Thailand), which

are common in the developing world. Without such constraints, those
groups lacking power (the "outsiders") will naturally mistrust executive
authority and these doubts about a government's aims can quickly boil
over into resentment or even violence against the regime. As the World
Bank notes, "social polarization undermines the accountability of government to citizens" and that lack of accountability means that politicians need not respond to the needs or interests of certain groups (World
Bank 2005, 320). *In fact, we find that when effective checks and balances
are missing from institutional arrangements, even rapid economic growth
may not save a democracy from reversal.* Indeed, our research highlights
that many recent examples of democratic backsliding have occurred in
high-growth nations (e.g., Russia, Thailand, and Venezuela).

Thus, it is not economic performance alone that determines the fate
of young democracies, as much of the earlier generation of literature in
political economy once argued (see Svolik 2007 for a review). Additionally, the institutional choices that societies make will also have a marked
influence on the prospects for democratic consolidation, irrespective of
how much growth a government manages to deliver during its mandate.
Further, the *type* of growth may matter as well; if all the benefits go into
only a few pockets, there may be little support for the economic policies of the day. As with political power, economic power also needs to
be redistributed if democracy is to consolidate. By examining both institutional and performance-related variables, our work therefore builds
on endogenous growth theory and the new institutionalism in seeking
deeper political and social correlates of why democratic regimes survive
or fail (see Landa and Kapstein 2001).

Beyond the domestic or internal choices that a new regime might
make with respect to its policies and institutions, the success of a young
democracy may also depend on the degree and kind of support it receives
from the international community. Although countries may "make their
own fates," as Larry Summers liked to say when he served as U.S. Treasury Secretary under President Bill Clinton, the international environment plays a more important role than is commonly appreciated. As we

will see, democracies that came into being anywhere in the world in the 1990s have had a much higher chance of survival than those that emerged in the 1960s, for reasons that we suspect have strongly to do with the incentives provided by the structure of contemporary world politics. An important question with respect to the future of democracy, therefore, might concern how changes in world politics – such as the relative rise of Chinese power, should that continue – will influence domestic regime choices in the developing world. Will the "China model" of authoritarian capitalism, the "Beijing Consensus," provide a compelling political-economic alternative to democracy? (See Ramo 2004 for a sympathetic view.)

In this examination of the relationship among institutions, economic performance, and democratic consolidation (and reversal), we tackle a large and growing academic literature while at the same time keeping our eyes fixed firmly on significant issues for public policy. With respect to the academic literature, we address in particular three leading hypotheses or pieces of "conventional wisdom" that have shaped much of the debate about the causes of democratic consolidation and reversal: *first,* that democratic reversal is primarily caused by poor economic performance; *second,* that presidential regimes are more likely to be reversed than parliamentary regimes; and *third,* that young democracies are more likely to be reversed than older democracies. Although each of these hypotheses has undoubtedly marshaled a fair amount of empirical support over the years, the present analysis, using our unique data set, suggests the need for some reconsideration.

From a policy-making perspective, this book places under the microscope the claim increasingly made by public officials that democratization *is a means for generating economic growth,* along with their associated belief that *economic growth is necessary for democratic consolidation.* As former United States Agency for International Development official David Yang has written, "Democratic governance is now seen [by the foreign assistance community] as not only an integral component of human development overall but also one of the main keys to unlocking socioeconomic progress in poorly performing countries" and he asserts that there is a *"new international consensus about the relationship between democracy and development..."* (Yang 2006, 377, italics added). Unfortunately, that consensus is not found among academics, and ironically much of the modern political economy literature has suggested that, to the contrary, democracy might even be detrimental to the economy over some relevant period of time (a case famously made by Olson 1982; for a focus on the poor performance of the world's youngest democracies, see Keefer 2007b).

Our research shows that newly democratic states are especially at risk of reversal during their first five years of existence, a crucial point that the international community needs to understand if it seeks to support their consolidation. As Samuel Huntington has written, these "new democracies are, in effect, in a catch-22 situation: lacking legitimacy they cannot become effective; lacking effectiveness they cannot develop legitimacy" (Huntington 1991, 258). Further, as Philip Keefer has stressed (Keefer 2007b), the leaders of young democracies – almost by definition – lack *credibility*; that is, voters and economic agents doubt their ability or willingness to craft, much less execute, policies that serve the general welfare. Therefore, building credibility and legitimacy (and doing so quickly!) is among the major challenges that the leaders of young democracies face if they are to consolidate their regimes.

How, then, are the world's youngest democracies faring in terms of their economic and political performance, and what factors explain the differences in performance that we observe? Why do some young democracies manage to consolidate, whereas others experience backsliding and even reversal? Are the leaders of newly democratic states willing and able to engage in the economic and institutional reforms that are necessary for long-run growth and democratic consolidation, or do short-term political pressures induce them to make "irresponsible" intertemporal choices? Finally, if the survival of young democracies is at risk, what can and should the foreign assistance community do to support them? These are among the questions that we address in this book.

It should be apparent that the topics we cover are at the core of contemporary debates over development policy. With the U.S. government's Millennium Challenge Corporation providing assistance only to democratic states (although its definition of democracy is somewhat elastic), and with the World Bank hammering away on the theme of "good governance," the institutional prerequisites of sustained growth have become central themes within the development community. Nonetheless, it has proved difficult for scholars and public officials alike to offer useful policy advice with respect to which institutions are most vital to developing countries and how these can be put into place. By identifying the "moving parts" within a government's institutional framework that are arguably of greatest importance to long-run growth and political stability, we try to make a contribution both to the development literature and to public policy.

We proceed with our study as follows. In the following chapter we examine the question of what makes young democracies different and thus "deserving" of special study, including their own data set! We examine that question through both theoretical and empirical lenses.

Next, we present descriptive statistics on how the young democracies have fared in practice, making use of our unique data set (which, among other things, is more up to date than the others cited herein, containing every episode of democratization that occurred between 1960 and 2004 and thus including, for example, the former Soviet Union). Additionally, using regression analysis, and specifically continuous time hazard models, we attempt to discern what, if any, characteristics differentiate young democracies that end in reversal (meaning that the democracy reverts to authoritarianism) from those that survive. Here we find that *although certain initial conditions like poverty, inequality, and ethnic fragmentation boost the likelihood that democracy will fail, institutional checks on the power of the executive can help to overcome these challenging circumstances and serve to promote policies that reconcile social conflicts over economic and political resources. Furthermore, where checks and balances are absent, and where public policies serve the few rather than the many via redistribution of income, assets, and/or opportunities, even relatively strong growth performance may not save a newly democratic state from reversal.*

As we will see, these are significant findings in that much of the prior literature has pointed to the alleged superiority of parliamentary over presidential systems in checking potential abuses of executive power, particularly within young democracies. We find, in contrast, that the extent to which parliamentary forms of government put into place the appropriate checks and balances is not clear. *The question of which institutional forms, along with such noninstitutional checks and balances as a free press, can best prevent the abuse of state power is of fundamental importance to democratic survival.* In short, what all this means is that a change of regime to democracy alone may be insufficient for addressing the deeper political and economic problems a given society faces.

Chapter 3 turns to case studies and discusses notable structural characteristics of newly democratic states in Latin America, Eastern Europe, Africa, and Asia, with an emphasis on why economic performance and regime survival rates have varied across these regions. We observe that credibility problems have frequently prompted politicians in Latin America to adopt shortsighted economic policies in the hope of generating rapid growth, whereas leaders in Africa, also lacking broad-based credibility, have generally resorted to patronage networks to build political support. In the post-Soviet bloc countries, we note the negative effects of resource endowments, notably oil, on political development in several states but also highlight the positive role played by European Union expansion in Eastern Europe in "locking-in" democracy. After discussing the diversity of experience among young democracies in Asia, we close with an analysis of the democratic experiments currently underway in Afghanistan and Iraq. Again, although we emphasize the role of structural factors or initial conditions in inducing certain types of institutions and policies, our data lead us to reject any form of determinism; after all, most of the young democracies that have successfully consolidated faced challenging initial conditions at the outset.

One factor that could conceivably facilitate democratic consolidation is foreign aid, and in Chapter 4 we assess the role of the international community in supporting the world's youngest democracies. Our view is that foreign assistance must be reconceptualized in such a way as to tighten the linkages between democracy promotion and economic policy by emphasizing the need for governments to distribute political and economic power. Within the aid regime today, however, democracy promoters try to build up political parties, institutions, and nongovernmental organizations on the one hand, whereas economists focus on what might generally be called *"Washington Consensus"* policies on the other, working mainly through technocrats who, they hope, can make decisions that are relatively independent of the particular government in power. As we will show, that hope may be forlorn – politics matters greatly to economic outcomes – and as a consequence these two arenas should become more closely aligned if donor nations are to help consolidate the world's youngest democratic states. The Millennium Challenge Corporation represents a promising model in that direction, although we express concern regarding some of its beliefs with respect to the political economy of development, as expressed by its "country compacts" with the nations where it has programs.

We conclude the book with a summary of our policy recommendations and our thoughts for further research. Clearly, there is much more work to be done and from a variety of methodological approaches (indeed, we hope our research, which makes use of different methodologies, encourages other scholars to do the same instead of relying on just one single approach). Appendices include a fuller discussion of our own methodology and list the cases of democratization that we analyzed.

We have accumulated heavy debts from many people during the long process of researching and writing this book, and we hope its publication provides at least partial thanks for the time and the ideas they shared with us. In particular, we must thank Nancy Birdsall, who as president of the Center for Global Development (CGD) has given this project an intellectual home and who has read every draft of the manuscript with great care. Similarly, Philip Keefer of the World Bank has not only inspired us through his scholarship but he also served as a sharp critic of several earlier drafts. Our thanks are also owed to Larry Diamond, who provided us with greatly needed early encouragement to pursue this study, along with a strong belief that it was worthy of foundation support. Additionally, we wish to thank participants at the June 2006 workshop on "Economic Foundations of Democratic Consolidation," held at the CGD, and to seminar participants at Duke University; the German Marshall Fund of the United States; the Institute for Defense and Strategic Studies of the National Technological University of Singapore; the Singapore Institute of International Affairs; the University of Texas; and the U.S. Department of State and National Intelligence Council for their comments on earlier drafts of the manuscript. We are also grateful to all those who participated in a small review session of our preliminary findings held at the CGD in October 2006, namely Verena Fritz of the Overseas Development Institute, Philip Keefer of the World Bank, and Joe Siegle of DAI, along with CGD colleagues Nancy Birdsall, Dennis DeTray, Stewart Patrick, and Liliana Rojas-Suarez; additional comments were provided by David Roodman of CGD. The book would not have been possible without an editor and publisher, and in John Berger of Cambridge University Press we were lucky to find an enthusiastic supporter of the project; the anonymous reviewers of the manuscript also gave us useful feedback that greatly improved the manuscript. The Smith Richardson Foundation provided the financial support to the CGD that made this project possible, for which we are most appreciative.

This book is dedicated to Professor Samuel P. Huntington, who is probably the most influential political scientist of the postwar era. Huntington's work has spanned nearly every subfield of political science, and among his lasting contributions are books on political order in developing societies (1968) and the "third wave" of democratization (1991).

We have learned much from his work, as the frequent citations here make abundantly clear. But beyond being a renowned scholar, Sam served as an incredibly generous mentor to Ethan B. Kapstein during many years at Harvard and long afterward, for which he is forever grateful.

1   What Makes Young Democracies Different?

It is generally accepted that young democracies are particularly likely to experience bad outcomes.

Philip Keefer (2007b)

RECENT YEARS HAVE SEEN A GROWING NUMBER OF ACAdemics and policy-makers express considerable optimism that democracy and economic growth are not only compatible but also mutually reinforcing. Democracy, for example, is alleged to provide investors with secure property rights, fostering growth that in turn strengthens domestic support for fledgling democratic institutions. As an example of this view, leading democracy scholar Larry Diamond (who, among other responsibilities, has served as a governance adviser in Iraq) recently told a group of African leaders that "Africa cannot develop without democracy," while further asserting that the academic literature points "clearly" to "*a causal effect* of democracy on economic growth..." (Diamond 2005, italics added).

As a consequence of that supposed causal relationship, he urged those who were gathered to shun any thoughts of adopting authoritarian solutions to their economic problems. Diamond said that the East Asian miracle, for example, "took place in a historic and regional context that is unlikely to be repeated" and that it therefore failed to provide a relevant developmental model for contemporary political leaders, despite continued growth in such countries as China and Singapore

(Diamond 2005). Democracy was not simply one path to development; apparently it was now the *only* path.

Diamond's line of argument stands in sharp contrast to a long tradition of research in political economy making precisely the opposite claim: namely that democracy and democratic institutions, including elections and powerful legislatures, provide political incentives that *undermine* long-run growth (for influential arguments, see Huntington 1968 on developing countries and Olson 1982 on the advanced industrial states). In fact, this older view is now enjoying something of a comeback, thanks to contemporary theoretical research that focuses on the microfoundations of political and economic behavior in developing countries. That work, along with at least some empirical analysis, points to a less optimistic picture of the relationship between democracy and development. As the World Bank has recently concluded, "Unfortunately, democratization does not ensure economic development" (World Bank 2005, 313).

With the jury still out with respect to how young democracies are faring in practice, we begin our examination of these regimes by asking the basic question of what makes them different from older, established governments and thus deserving of "special" academic treatment and policy attention. We focus on five points.

First, many young democracies emerge in the presence of challenging initial conditions such as widespread poverty and inequality, economic dependence on a small range of commodities, and high levels of ethnic fragmentation among other social divisions. Modernization theorists (in a sense going back to Aristotle) would argue that these conditions, such as a poor and uneducated population, make it much more difficult for democracy to take root (Lipset 1959). The countries in our data set, for example, launched their democratic episodes with an average initial per-capita income of just over $1,800 in 2006 dollars. Moreover, as Figure 1.1 demonstrates, the distribution of these countries is skewed toward the poorer end of the spectrum, so the median income per capita is $850. On average, the countries that underwent democratization during the

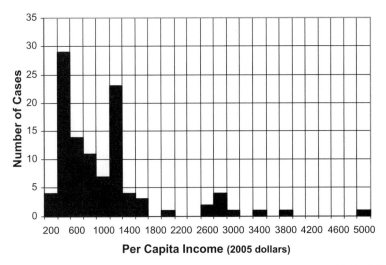

FIGURE 1.1. Per Capita Incomes of New Democracies, 1960–2004.
Source: WDI, authors' calculations.

period under analysis (1960–2004) have had a poverty rate of just over 20 percent of the population living on less than one dollar per day and over 40 percent living on less than two dollars per day. Given these economic conditions, the first task of a young democracy might be to try and relieve poverty quickly, thus leading to policies that may undermine the foundations for long-run economic growth and possibly democratic consolidation as well.

Second, given these initial conditions, the leaders of young democracies may have difficulty making credible promises to a broad range of constituents, as Keefer has so powerfully argued (Keefer 2007a, 2007b). In deeply divided societies, where asset inequality, ethnic fragmentation, and other divisions (including divisions among elites) have been exploited by previous leaders to advance their own careers, trust may be lacking across social groups. Ironically, efforts by politicians to build such trust may lead them to pursue perverse policies. For example, leaders may rely on clientelistic or patrimonial policies, creating an insider/outsider dichotomy; alternatively, populism may be the order of the day, with economic outcomes like high levels of inflation that end up taxing the poor. The net result is that politicians lack credibility (people do not believe that they can deliver on their promises) and legitimacy (meaning that the government is not viewed as being truly representative). And without credibility and legitimacy, it is difficult if not impossible for the young democracy to consolidate.

Unfortunately for young democracies, credibility takes time to build, as governments engage in repeated transactions with the voting public. But politicians may never have the luxury of time, given the overwhelming economic and political pressures they face to take action. If these actions are not viewed as welfare enhancing, however, the regime will have trouble sustaining itself as a democracy.

Third, and related, young democracies are likely to be characterized by institutional weaknesses, including ineffectual political parties and an absence of effective checks and balances on the chief executive (World Bank 2005). Again, by definition, institutions take time to build and to develop credibility and legitimacy. Central banks need to maintain stable monetary policies over time if they are to establish their inflation-fighting credentials and judicial authorities need time to establish their independence. Parliaments and executives must shape their roles and responsibilities so as to forge a power-sharing arrangement that works. Political parties take time to form and to coalesce around particular themes that aggregate the interests of their constituents, and these parties must also "learn" how to serve democracy by sitting in responsible opposition to the government of the day. Most important, these institutions must interact in such a way as to prevent the concentration of political and economic power: we show that the absence of effective checks and balances is among the most powerful predictors of democratic failure.

Fourth, the political and economic performance of young democratizers is much more volatile as a group than the political and economic performance of older democratic states. There are larger swings in such economic variables as inflation, and there are higher chances of democratic collapse. Separating these volatile states into a separate data set and comparing their experience with that of older democracies might therefore reveal something about their particular pathologies.

Fifth, and finally, the international system weighs more heavily on young democracies than on older democratic states, for better and for worse. These states are more likely to receive foreign aid, which could put specific pressures on their political economy, and they could also be candidates for membership in regional and/or international organizations, requiring them to adopt certain policies if not institutions in order to qualify for accession. As commodity exporters, the international economy could play a more decisive role in shaping their performance, while the rules and regulations of the trade regime could open and close doors to their export sectors, again with significant economic consequences. Most dramatically, democracy may have been imposed on some of these countries by a foreign power (as in Afghanistan and Iraq), and perhaps its maintenance requires the presence of foreign troops.

What these five points suggest is that the fate of young democracies is somehow shaped by the interaction of initial conditions, political institutions, economic performance, and the international community. But we now need to move beyond this "laundry list" in order to make our analysis tractable. Accordingly, in this chapter we begin by asking how the introduction of democracy in the developing world might be expected to influence economic performance from a theoretical standpoint before looking at some empirical evidence on this topic. We concentrate on that particular linkage because, if the academic community agrees on one general proposition with respect to the world's wide array of young democracies, it is probably that their consolidation depends mainly on their economic performance.

As we describe in what follows, there are several distinct institutional pathways that forge a link between a democracy's political arrangements and its economy, influencing in turn its chances for consolidation or collapse.

- First, democracy as a political system may influence the economy directly via the electoral process to the extent that the process induces politicians to favor or adopt policies that please the voting public;
- Second, and related, the linkage between politics and economics may be channeled through political parties, which are supposed to aggregate the interests of voters who prefer particular sets of policies;
- Third, the institutional arrangements that a democracy adopts – for example, whether it is presidential or parliamentary – may have a decisive influence on the types of economic policies that are adopted.

Overall, these three interlocking attributes of a democracy – its electoral system (who gets to vote and which offices are elected), its political parties (how many and which interests are aggregated), and its institutions (what type) – define its constitutional political economy and will help to determine whether governments will be formed and policies implemented that induce agents to engage in productive behavior that furthers democratic consolidation.

We recognize that democratic consolidation requires more than the holding of elections, the founding of political parties, and/or the writing of a constitution. In addition to these institutional factors, many *non*institutional changes are necessary to guarantee the internalization of democratic values and the emergence of what the policy-making community refers to as "good governance," including secure property rights, stable monetary and fiscal policies, and other incentives for long-term investment that promotes sustainable growth. Nonetheless, in considering a nation's constitutional political economy and its evolution during the early years of democracy, we will leave to the side the noninstitutional factors whose influence might be equally if not even more significant for a nation's well-being. For example, *liberal* democracies have many specific attributes – for example, a respect for civil liberties and a free press – that could be of great long-run importance by encouraging, if only indirectly, greater individual creativity and risk-taking.[1] So-called social capital has been often cited as playing a role in boosting both economic performance and governance arrangements, because it provides the trust or cement that enables people to engage in arm's length or anonymous, contractual transactions, which are crucial to the long-run development of a market economy and functioning polity. Democratic governments may also have different *ideas* about economic policy, and those ideas or ideologies could have an independent influence on performance; some countries, for example, may believe that fairness or social justice entails greater income redistribution, whereas others hold it entails greater access to opportunities. These aspects of modern democratic states (i.e., their nongovernmental institutions and their ideas about economic policy) among many others deserve much more attention than we can provide in this brief study.

Voters, Elections, and Economic Policy

If democracies share any fundamental trait, it is the presence of regular, contested elections for public office. In many respects these elections form the core of political life and serve as generators of tremendous civic engagement. But that is not all: the electoral process also reverberates throughout a nation's economy – and perhaps even more so in young democratizers, as opposed to the older industrial states, for good and for ill – via a number of distinctive channels that we trace in this section.

---

[1] Following the tradition made famous by Drucker in his classic 1939 *End of Economic Man* as well as Friedrich von Hayek and the Austrian School more generally, the Nobel Prize winner Douglass North (1990) has argued that markets function more efficiently in democratic societies due to the personal freedom they allow economic agents. In a similar vein, Amartya Sen has suggested that freer flows of information have prevented famines from occurring under democratic governments (Sen 1994). We note, however, that liberal institutions of this type may be lacking in many young democracies, given that they make take time to develop.

As we will see, for many years scholars have suggested that the competitive, electoral process associated with democracy leads to a number of ill effects, such as budget deficits and redistributive income policies that reduce private investment and growth; thus democracy might not make sense for poor, developing countries that simply could not afford the luxury of dampening growth rates that were already below their optimal paths (Huntington 1968; Rao 1984). However, research has also suggested that political competition could bring a number of economic benefits to democratizers, such as more and better public goods and less corruption. In this section, we first discuss some of the positive impacts of the electoral process on economic policy and performance in young democracies before examining several possible negative effects. Again, if economic performance reflects a government's institutions and policies, we need to relate the two in a deeper way in order to understand why some democracies consolidate while others fail.

To begin with, the holding of contested elections can enhance efficiency and boost growth in several ways.

First, by putting into place a mechanism for accountability – namely the possibility that elected officials will be voted out of office at the end of the term if they perform badly or fail to live up to their promises – elections discipline the temptation to engage in welfare-reducing policies. Whereas an autocrat can arbitrarily expropriate property for his own benefit, the accountability introduced by periodic elections provides a check on this power, leading to stronger property rights, greater economic efficiency, and less uncertainty (North 1990). Bardhan and Yang state the case clearly: "political competition disciplines an incumbent from claiming too much of the economic pie for himself" (Bardhan and Yang 2004, 5), for if he does so, he will be voted out of office.

Second, by generating incentives for groups with opposing policy positions to compromise, elections can ameliorate conflict and promote policy stability. This feature of elections may be particularly important in young democracies in which social or ethnic divisions loom large.

Rodrik (1999, 2000), for example, has elaborated a model in which two groups with divergent policy preferences interact repeatedly to formulate policy. If the groups face uncertainty about which among them will have a superior bargaining position in the future, say through the election of their preferred candidate, they can reach an equilibrium in which they compromise over policy today. By introducing such uncertainty over outcomes through competitive elections, democracy promotes compromise, reducing policy volatility and facilitating better economic performance. Bunce similarly observes that democracy combines "uncertain outcomes with certain procedures," providing the background conditions that inform and motivate economic risk-taking (Bunce 2001, 52).

Third, by introducing competitive pressures into the public sector, democracy provides yet another check on rent-seeking, albeit indirectly, and so improves efficiency. Lake and Baum (2001) lay out a theoretical model in which, in an initial setting, the government is a monopoly provider of public services and as a consequence acts to restrict supply to drive up price in the form of rents or corruption extracted by government officials. With this setting as background, they view the introduction of democracy as a way of rendering the market for public services "contestable," with candidates for political office being potential entrants threatening to undercut the monopoly provider. In short, by introducing competitive pressures into the public sector, democracy has the potential to force the state to supply more and better public services, and even in young democracies it appears that a rapid improvement in the provision and quality of public services often takes place.[2]

---

[2] This argument, it will be observed, rings of the fiscal federalism literature which argues that federalist systems are efficiency-enhancing because economic agents can vote with their feet and move, forcing local governors to restrain their personal rent-seeking and provide the public services that people actually want. Again, questions may be raised about the benefits of political decentralization in those developing countries where the central government is already too weak to provide many of the public goods that citizens demand.

When Lake and Baum (2001) test their model empirically, they find that public goods provision is not only greater in democracies but also is generally qualitatively superior to that in less democratic countries. In cross sectional regressions, they find that higher levels of democracy are associated with better education, as measured by a host of indicators, including literacy, primary school student/teacher ratios, and the level of enrollment at all grades, and with better health, as measured by life expectancy, mortality, inoculations, and population per physician, as well as access to healthcare and clean water. They also run time series cross sectional regressions and find that an increase in a given country's level of democracy results in a statistically significant and rapid jump in public service provision.

These results are also supported by descriptive statistics included in Papaioannou and Siourounis (2004), indicating that democratization yields rapid increases in life expectancy and schooling. Likewise, Tavares and Wacziarg (2001) find that higher levels of democracy are associated with higher average years of secondary schooling. Keefer (2005) also finds that longer periods of uninterrupted democracy are characterized by higher average secondary school enrollment, further bolstering the claim that democracy is associated with better public service provision. In short, there is some evidence that young democracies do, in fact, respond to voter demands for more public goods. However, Kapstein (2004) finds that the higher the degree of ethnic fragmentation, the fewer the public goods, as measured by infant mortality rates and years of education. Again, to the extent that democracies deliver more public goods, that generalization may mask important differences among young democratic states.

The premise that elections can promote good economic policy and induce the provision of public investment is predicated on a crucial assumption: that politicians are able and willing to make *credible promises* to voters. But as Keefer (2007b) has argued, such credibility is likely to be in short supply, especially in countries that are sharply divided along income, ethnic, or other lines – as is the case in many developing world settings. In such cases, politicians may instead be forced to engage in clientelistic behavior to build political support, providing targeted goods to core allies (e.g., particular geographic areas, or members of the same clan or ethnic group) and undersupplying public goods. Where clientelism is the *modus operandi*, "outsiders" can get what they want only through corruption or other noninstitutional means. Such societies may be more violent or at least less stable. In short, they will be less capable of delivering long-run economic growth.

Developing credibility is, for Keefer, the key challenge facing the leaders of young democracies. By definition, such credibility can arise only through *repeated interactions* between voters and candidates, between branches of government, and among political parties – interactions that serve to build confidence and trust in the new political system among the polity as a whole. As a consequence, it may take many years to create the socioeconomic and political foundations of policy credibility. Under what conditions do credible politicians and institutions emerge? That unanswered question is of crucial importance; indeed, discovering how the social norms of cooperation develop over time to encompass entire polities – what Elster (1989) has called the "cement of society" – may prove the ultimate key to understanding long-run growth (Landa and Kapstein 2001).

Keefer's discussion of credibility raises some of the deeper causal factors that may, in fact, promote *bad* policies and outcomes in young democracies, as opposed to the good ones that some theory and evidence promise. Given a lack of credibility with the voting public, politicians will either target certain constituents or will promote policies that are at best "short-term" fixes in an effort to win elections and stay in power. Moreover, economists have long observed that periodic elections give elected officials an incentive to pursue policies that improve economic performance only in the period prior to voting. This may lead politicians to stimulate the economy artificially by printing money and abandoning fiscal rectitude during the run-up to elections in the hope of convincing the median voter of their skill in managing the economy. Indeed, in both industrial and developing countries, rising levels of inflation and government deficits in the preelection period seem widespread, though the situation appears especially acute in the developing world. (Brender and Drazen 2004; for an alternative view, see Kaplan 2006).

Specifically, political business cycle (PBC) theory postulates that incumbent leaders, irrespective of ideology, will be tempted to use policy to stimulate the economy by loosening fiscal and monetary policy in the run-up to elections in order to convince voters of their superior ability to generate jobs and growth.[3] Block (2002, 6) notes that PBC theories implicitly assume competitive elections, in which a degree of uncertainty exists regarding the outcome – a leader who will certainly be reelected has no reason to signal his managerial competence by stimulating the economy. By implication, a shift from a less democratic government to a more democratic government with greater contestation of public offices implies that PBCs will appear or be magnified in newly democratizing countries. This intuition is confirmed by various empirical investigations.

Block (2002) finds that political budget cycles[4] are indeed observed only in countries with competitive elections. On the assumption that

---

[3] Here we focus on opportunistic PBC theories. Partisan PBC models see politically determined fluctuations as a result of the different preferences of left- and right-wing parties for unemployment and inflation (Alesina et al. 1997, 45). Given that the left–right dichotomy outlined by partisan PBC theory assumes a political landscape approximating that of Western Europe and North America, opportunistic PBC theory appears a more appropriate framework for analyzing young democracies, most of which are in transition and developing countries where the party system is often weak and where presidential systems are widespread (Block, Ferree, and Singh 2003).

[4] While the theory of PBCs suggests that politicians will attempt to manipulate growth to further their chances of reelection, in practice their ability to do this may be severely limited, particularly in developing countries. It is thus unsurprising that while numerous studies have found evidence of opportunistic PBCs in developing countries in inflation, money supply growth, government spending, no studies have found that PBCs in developing countries cause growth to change in the periods before or after elections. For example, Schuknecht (1996) finds no association between election periods and changes in output growth. Similarly, in a study of African economies, Block, Ferree, and Singh (2003) mention in passing that they find no association between multi-party or founding elections and growth.

leaders facing reelection will boost current expenditure, which tends to more immediately benefit voters, Block tests current expenditure as a share of total central government expenditure increases in election years.[5] He finds that such increases occur but only in countries with competitive elections. *A shift from dictatorship to democracy therefore appears to imply the emergence of a political budget cycle.*

Whereas Block (2002) compares democratic and nondemocratic regimes, Block, Ferree, and Singh (2003) contrast new democracies with more established ones and find that political budget cycles are more pronounced in the former. They find that competitive elections in new democracies do increase public spending and that this impact is amplified when the election is the first competitive election after a period of noncompetitive or no elections. Moreover, such "founding elections" are associated with acceleration of the growth of the money supply. They outline a number of reasons why PBCs might be more pronounced in new democracies. Not only do incumbents who have not been competitively elected likely to have more discretion to manipulate the economy, but such leaders have an incentive to fend off any challengers early to minimize future competition (Block, Ferree and Singh 2003).

The association between new democracies and political business cycles is confirmed by Brender and Drazen (2004), who find that PBCs are present *only* in newly democratic states. In a sample of 68 democracies from 1960 to 2001, they find that if the sample is narrowed to exclude the first four elections following democratization, all traces of a PBC disappear. By contrast, election-year dummies are significantly associated

---

[5] Interestingly, whereas Keefer (2005) finds that the proportion of public spending devoted to investment will fall as democracies mature, Block (2002) finds evidence that electoral contestation is associated with a fall in public investment as a share of Gross Domestic Product (GDP). These results are not necessarily contradictory, since investment as a share of the government budget may rise while falling as a percentage of GDP. Nonetheless, their logic conflicts on a theoretical level: Keefer views public investment as a prime avenue for clientelistic channeling of jobs and money to supporters, whereas Block sees current expenditure as the easiest way to direct public resources to supporters.

with higher deficits and greater expenditure during the first four elections following democratization. Including separate dummy variables for the first, second, third, and fourth elections following democratization shows that the significance of the election year declines as the democracy ages.

Thus, previous studies of the PBC suggest that new democracies will undergo an increase in the variability of rates of inflation and money supply growth and in the level and composition of government spending. In addition to the disruptions that these variations cause, they will also likely retard growth in the years after democratization by increasing economic volatility.[6] Consequently, the presence of PBCs in new democracies, with the concomitantly higher volatility of monetary and fiscal variables and the resulting slower growth, suggests that new democracies may face particular challenges in the formulation of economic policy and in turn to regime consolidation. Lacking credibility, or facing a demand for quick action, politicians face intertemporal trade-offs in which short-term remedies undermine the long-term foundations of sustained growth.

Analysis of our own data set provides qualified support for these general findings. At first glance, inflation in our sample appears to double, jumping from an average annual rate of 80 percent to 165 percent in the five years before and after democratization. But these numbers hide some important cross-country differences, and it must be emphasized that average inflation in young democracies improved relative to the previous authoritarian period in around 30 percent of the cases. Still, as we report in our regression analysis in the following chapter, inflation is a significant predictor of democratic reversal.

With respect to government spending, our data show little difference between young democracies and the preceding authoritarian regimes.

---

[6] Ramey and Ramey (1995, 1148) note that volatility in precisely the variables affected by the PBC – monetary growth and fiscal policy – significantly lowers growth. Exploring this relationship in detail, Aizenman and Marion (1999) find that volatility in these variables is associated with lower private investment, which presumably causes the lower growth found by Ramey and Ramey (1992).

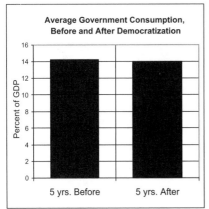
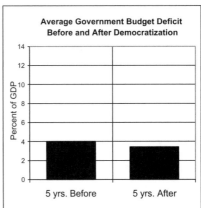

FIGURE 1.2. Government Spending in New Democracies. *Source:* WDI,
IFS, and authors' calculations.

Average government consumption in the countries in our data set was
basically unchanged in the five years before and after democratization,
remaining at 14.2 percent of GDP (see Figure 1.2). Further, the average
budget deficit in the five years after democratization is not significantly
different from the average deficit in the five years prior to democratization. Still, averages hide important differences across regions, which we
discuss in more detail in later chapters.

Intriguingly, differences in political participation across democracies
may also be a factor in determining the level of government spending. For example, Plümper and Martin find that government spending
in countries with a "medium degree of political participation" (which
they define as those that are considered democratic but do not achieve
the highest score possible on indices of democracy) is about two percent lower than government spending in either "pure" autocracies or
"pure" democracies (meaning countries which receive the highest possible scores in those categories; see Plümper and Martin 2004, 40). For
now, we can say that differences *between* democracies may prevent us
from making general predictions about whether government spending
will increase or decrease following a transition from authoritarian rule.

In the previous paragraphs, the underlying assumption is not only that elections matter but also that self-interested voters, who cast a watchful eye over rent-seeking and other welfare-reducing policies, can determine election results. On one level, that seems like a sensible way to conceptualize the electorate, but the reality may be more complex for a variety of reasons. Democratic electoral theory, for example, has traditionally emphasized the power of the *median voter*, whose support must be gained in a divided polity if a politician is to be elected to office (Downs 1957). By definition, the median voter, who occupies the fifth and sixth income deciles, owns less capital than the average for the nation as a whole or, to put this in the starkest terms, we might say that the median voter is poorer than the average voter. *This fact is consequential for economic policy and performance, for it suggests that the median voter, whose political support is decisive in contested elections, will demand income redistribution from the rich to herself as the price of the political support she gives her representatives* (Meltzer and Richard 1981).

Unfortunately, these demands for redistribution give those who possess wealth in a democracy (i.e., the rich) less incentive to save and to invest (because any profits will be in part redistributed to the broader citizenry), and they may even decide to take their capital to friendlier locales like tax havens, leaving the country poorer. One frequently posited outcome of this interaction between rich and poor is that democracies must inevitably emphasize short-run consumption at the expense of long-run investment, with the result that a country's growth potential goes unfulfilled (Huntington 1968; Rao 1984). The economic policies of democracies are thus posited to be redistributive toward the nonelite (i.e., toward the median voter), and growth is negatively affected as a consequence.

Recent work in modern political economy has viewed the median voter's preference for redistribution as driving not only policy choices within democracies, *but even more fundamentally as being decisive in terms of whether democracy actually takes root in a given country in the first place.* Acemoglu and Robinson (2006), for example, model democracy as the outcome of a redistributive "game" between elites (the rich) and nonelites (the "citizens" or the poor). In the absence of redistribution, the poor threaten revolution; but when too much redistribution is demanded, the elites threaten coups (or, in the era of globalization, massive capital flight). By giving up their monopoly on the franchise, the elites try to guarantee their security and their property rights in return for the partial redistribution that they know will occur once the poor can vote over public policies. The poor, however, see democratic institutions as a bulwark against attempts by the elite to retake power by force and therefore act prudently in the interest of maintaining this regime type (Acemoglu and Robinson 2006). *The critical point is that central to democratic politics is social conflict over how the economic pie gets distributed. If that is true, it suggests a policy lesson of vital importance, namely that growth alone may not ensure the survival of a young democratic polity in the absence of positive, redistributive measures that respond to voter demands.*

Academic models that emphasize the influence of the median voter on economic policy have won a prized spot in the political economy pantheon, but clearly the preferences of the median voter do not seem to be automatically translated into policy, either in industrial or developing countries. Indeed, focusing on government spending that explicitly seeks to redistribute income, Mello and Tiongson (2006) find that higher inequality is significantly associated with *lower* government transfers as a share of GDP. This finding is corroborated by Allcott, Lederman, and López (2006), who hypothesize that higher inequality results in greater influence over economic policy for the wealthy (as the rich get richer they also get more power). Kapstein and Milanovic (2003) suggest that to the extent that redistribution does take place, it does not direct government spending to the poor in general but rather to key political groups.[7]

---

[7] We would expect this to be especially the case in countries with strong presidential regimes, which are hypothesized to favor targeted expenditures, as in Latin America or Eastern Europe. We are unaware of any studies that examine the variation in social safety nets in terms of regime type in the context of developing countries.

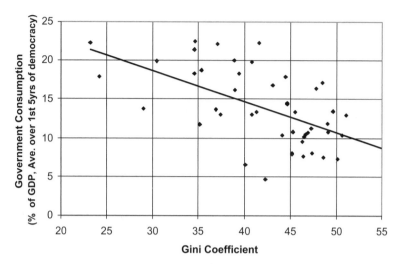

FIGURE 1.3. Inequality and Government Consumption in New Democracies. *Source:* WDI, UTIP, authors' calculations.

Using our own data set, in contrast, we do find some evidence of government spending motivated by a desire for redistribution of income. Figure 1.3 plots the relationship between income inequality (as measured by the Gini coefficient) and average government consumption as a proportion of GDP in five years following democratization. The relationship is in fact negative (the correlation coefficient is −0.59), providing some support for the idea that inequality prompts higher government spending.

Beyond the data, we note there are some dramatic country cases in which redistributive measures have been or are being put into place. The democratically elected government of South Africa, for example, has launched Black Economic Empowerment programs whose ultimate objectives are asset, income, and opportunity redistribution for the racial victims of apartheid, whereas Brazil – another extremely unequal country – has also launched a number of programs aimed at eradicating hunger, such as *Bolsa Familia*, and keeping poor youth in school, like the famous *Bolsa Escola*. These extensive programs do suggest serious attempts to help uplift societies' poorest citizens, but it remains questionable whether they will reduce income and asset inequality in a meaningful way over a relevant time horizon. To the extent the data are available, they suggest that the income distribution, as measured by the Gini coefficient, remains relatively sticky around the world for long periods of time.

To advocates of collective choice theory, the absence of compelling evidence in favor of large-scale redistribution in democratic polities would not be surprising. In perhaps the most famous critique of the median voter model, Mancur Olson questioned the ability of individuals to advance their material interests effectively in electoral among other settings, given the free-rider temptation in the face of collective goods provision (Olson 1965, 1982). Although a majority of voters might favor a particular policy, for example, few may bother to take the time and make the effort to go out and vote (to say nothing of convincing like-minded others to go to the polling station) if the gains from that policy are small for any one person. Because individuals face severe organizational impediments and are tempted to free-ride – impediments and temptations which we can assume are even all the greater in predominantly rural developing countries – their political impact might not be very great after all as compared to that of organized interests. Olson suggested instead that small groups with a shared purpose would be most successful in advancing their political and economic agenda to the extent they had a strong material interest in a particular policy outcome, because they would be willing to invest in the effort needed to influence politicians. He further asserted that such lobbies have played an extremely negative role in the economic performance of nations; in fact, he assigned them a central role in the economic decline of the older democratic states (Olson 1982).

For Olson, it was organized interest groups that prevented politicians from implementing welfare-enhancing changes and reforms, like the move to free trade. Interestingly, this model may prove illuminating for young democracies as well. Hellman, for example, has applied a similar perspective to Russia's post-communist economic reforms, demonstrating how well-organized groups (often former Soviet officials) effectively captured the economic reform process during the early 1990s, blocking those reforms that would have led to more openness and competition (Hellman 1998). As a consequence, they won a windfall for themselves through, for example, "voucher" privatization in which foreign firms were not allowed to buy up shares in certain industries. Russia's new billionaires are largely the product of this process of "partial" reform, and it is troubling in this context that Russia is among those countries whose democracy has reversed; its rating by Freedom House, for example, has recently gone backward to "not free." More generally, the power of special interests across the developing world is exemplified, *inter alia,* by relatively high tariff barriers that serve to protect noncompetitive domestic industries. The quasi-monopolistic prices that these producers capture for their goods and services, in turn, undermine the buying power of the poor and increase inequality. More generally, such policies reduce economic welfare and the possibility of redistribution to the poor, and thus may play a role in democratic reversal.

To summarize, one of the central characteristics of democracy is its reliance on competitive elections for choosing political leaders who are accountable to voters. This accountability has the potential to check abuses by elected officials and improve the quality of governance. But the holding of elections also introduces incentives for elected officials to engage in pernicious behavior, including manipulating the economy for electoral gain. Further, where politicians lack credibility and legitimacy with the electorate as a whole, they will turn to either clientelistic policies that only target key supporters or to inflationary policies that reflect a need to broaden their appeal by printing money. Such policies will reduce welfare and meaningful redistribution, thus undermining support for newly established democratic regimes.

Political Parties and Economic Policy

In democratic states, political parties generally play the central role in organizing groups of voters with similar interests. They can also serve

to enhance the credibility of any one candidate for office by linking a
number of politicians with voters through a common platform. Further,
by sitting in opposition to the government of the day, they act as a crucial
check on executive power and as overseers of the policy process; as two
scholars of East Asian politics have recently put it, democracy can only
flourish when "states allow and in fact have a valid, working and worthy
political opposition" (Tay and Lay Hwee 2006, 27).

   This section explores, admittedly in broad-brush fashion, whether the
political parties found in the young democracies of the developing world
are serving any of these purposes at the present time and what the consequences are of party structure and behavior for regime consolidation
or reversal. We find that the state of the party system in most young
democracies is not good. As the expert in this area, Thomas Carothers,
reports after an exhaustive survey, most parties "are what might be called
political cabals or clubs – highly personalistic, leader-centric organizations in which an assertive, ambitious, often charismatic party leaders,
together with a set of closer followers and associates, pursue political power through elections" (Carothers 2006, 6). This is not surprising; to the extent that leaders lack widespread credibility and legitimacy, they effectively end up building small, tightly knit organizations of
"insiders."

   Before discussing the consequences of party organization in the
developing world, it is crucial to emphasize (at the risk of stating the
obvious) that the *number* and *type* of parties that are permitted by constitutional authority to stand in an election and take power may also
be of crucial importance to democratic consolidation and reversal. In
a recent paper for example, Joseph Wright (2008) has challenged long-
held notions that political competition ought to be limited in early years
to help stabilize fragile polities. Thus it has been argued by scholars
and policy-makers alike that "extremist" parties must not be allowed
to participate in (much less win) elections because they would only
use their authority to impose an illiberal regime on society. Wright, in
contrast, finds that "new democracies with low levels of initial political

competition are likely to fail" for the straightforward reason that aggrieved groups will challenge the regime using extraconstitutional means
(Wright 2008, 1). Wright's analysis reminds us that political parties left
outside the electoral process may be more dangerous than those that
actively participate, irrespective of their particular platform.

How do parties serve the electorate? There is a long-standing tradition in the political economy literature, called the "partisanship school,"
that links political parties with well-defined approaches to economic policy (for reviews, see Jackman 1986; Drazen 2001; Rueda 2001). Briefly,
the partisanship school holds that "each party takes a distinctive policy
position that includes a known program" (Jackman 1986, 135). Specifically, left-wing or social democratic governments will protect the interests of labor and the working class, whereas right-wing or conservative governments will protect the interests of those who have accumulated capital. Parties serve to aggregate interests in such a way as to win
elections, and once in power they become vehicles for advancing a particular economic program. These contrasting approaches to economic policy are allegedly made manifest in macroeconomic performance, with
social democracies having higher levels of taxation, government spending, and inflation than conservative governments.

As Rueda (2001) notes, critical to the partisanship school's model is
the assumption that political parties have "core constituencies" whose
interests are paramount in setting the platform and in policy-making
should the party form a government. A party's main challenge, therefore, is to build a "winning coalition" around this core constituency. If
the party follows solely the preferences of its core, however, it may well
lose election after election (that, of course, *could* be a perverse outcome
of internal party politics). Parties must therefore achieve the right balance if they are to win elections. On the one hand, although the winning
strategy of coalition-building may temper the more extreme strands of
a given economic strategy, on the other, the overall policy trajectory
nonetheless remains clear to voters, at least in contrast to that of the rival
party. Thus, parties must provide voters with clear choices. Note how this

interpretation of electoral politics differs from models in which median voters drive both parties toward similarly convergent policy stances.

It must be emphasized that the partisanship approach to the relationship between politics and economic policy is firmly materialistic in that it associates core constituencies with the "class struggle." Jackman (1986) believes the evidence for this is weak and thus considers the model "wanting." Although he doubts "that parties are fundamentally motivated by programmatic concerns," it may simply be the case that political scientists have focused too much on *economic concerns* as opposed to other voter preoccupations (Jackman 1986, 143). Numerous pundits, for example, have asserted that it has been the genius of the Republican Party in the United States to win middle- and lower-class votes in several recent elections while pursuing economic policies detrimental to their interests by appealing primarily to "values" as opposed to the pocketbook (for a cogent analysis, see Frank 2004).

Is partisanship of this kind also relevant in the setting of developing countries? More generally, what functions do political parties serve in young democracies? Do they act as theories drawn from industrial world experience would suggest? As we will see, there are reasons why the study of political parties might need revisiting in the context of the young democratizers of the developing world, and in fact we believe research along these lines is of critical importance to our understanding of the institutional correlates of long-run democratic consolidation.

For example, so far as we are aware, the partisanship school has not applied its model of party behavior to other identifiable constituencies, such as the religious or ethnic groups that are currently prominent in many developing countries. A recent case in which such constituencies played an important role in electoral politics is the 2006 parliamentary election in Iraq, in which political parties were basically identified with groups such as Sunni and Shiite Muslims and the Kurds. We note that the effects of these party groupings on economic policy and performance have been little studied; Haggard and Kaufman (1995), for example, relied on traditional, class-based partisanship models in their analysis of the political economy of democratic transitions. But given the seeming importance of religious or ethnic politics in many countries, this seems a major gap in the party literature as it applies to many young democratizers; surely, this is an area that should attract more research from social scientists and policy-makers in the years ahead.

Still other theorists have emphasized that the ideological orientation of the political party in power matters less than the level of institutionalization that characterizes the parties that compete for office. As already noted, established parties are crucial to public policy-making in democracies because they can help provide politicians with credibility (Keefer 2007b). An individual politician, particularly in a young democracy, is likely to have a hard time convincing voters that she will fulfill her promises once elected to office. Lodged within a programmatic party, however, voters may have greater confidence in the ability of their politicians to shape and execute policy choices. Empirical work on this question supports the contention that strong parties improve the quality of policy-making. In their study of the political economy of economic reform in 13 countries, for example, Williamson and Haggard (1994) reject the idea that right-wing governments are better suited or even more likely to implement market-oriented reforms. Instead, they find that the governments are more likely to carry out economic reforms when the party in power enjoys a broad support base, irrespective of its ideology.

Similarly, Haggard and Kaufman stress the crucial importance of parties that are capable of channeling social conflicts over such issues as income distribution and the knitting of safety nets for the formulation of high-quality economic policy, and they conclude that broad-based, cohesive political parties (or stable coalitions of parties) are particularly suited to perform this function. In contrast, they find that fragmented or polarized party systems generally fail to implement welfare-enhancing economic policies (Haggard and Kaufman 1995). *As we will see later, the positive role of strong, credible parties in keeping their economic promises has led many scholars to suggest that parliamentary democracies are a superior institutional form when it comes to delivering political stability to young and fragile democratic states, particularly during times of economic crisis when they are most likely to be threatened by reversal.* Again, however, we note Wright's (2008) warning that by limiting political competition and the number of parties that are allowed to compete in elections, regimes risk a violent backlash from the aggrieved.

Analyses from a variety of theoretical perspectives thus suggest that coherent political parties will improve the quality of economic policy and performance in democratic states, increasing the chances that a given democracy will survive. From this perspective, it is particularly troubling to find that such parties rarely exist in today's young democracies. Carothers reports that

> citizens of almost every struggling or new democracy are deeply unhappy with their political parties...parties are perceived as corrupt, self-interested organizations that relentlessly work to maximize their own welfare with no real concern for ordinary citizens. They are seen as elitist organizations run by self-appointed leaders who are in politics out of greed and ambition. Citizens see little real difference among the main parties in their countries; the parties do not seem to stand for anything and whatever ideological labels are affixed to the parties are either just historical holdovers or empty symbols. (Carothers 2004, 3)

He concludes from his survey results that

> Given the central functions that parties are supposed to play in a democracy, the weak state of parties in many developing and post-communist countries is a serious problem for democratization. *Above all, the shaky state of parties contributes significantly to the inadequate aggregation and representation of interests which is such a debilitating problem in so many new and struggling democracies.* (Carothers 2004, 3–4; italics added)

From the standpoint of economic policy, and of a country's subsequent chances for democratic consolidation, that failure may be

particularly grave (but for a somewhat more optimistic view of party politics from an African perspective, see Carbone 2003; note that this analysis was written before the contested elections in Kenya of December
2007). A party disconnected from its electoral base, which fails to aggregate and represent the interests of its supposed constituents, is unlikely to
govern effectively when and if it achieves power. Without the credibility
afforded by strong parties, both executives – presidents or prime minis-
ters – and legislators will be much more prone to engage in the negative
behaviors discussed in the previous section of this chapter, such as pursuing policies that sacrifice medium-term growth in favor of short-term
consumption or engineering political business cycles.

Furthermore, when parties sit in opposition, they can play a critical
monitoring role in preventing abuses by the leadership – a function that
we believe to be crucial to good economic performance in young democratic states. Weak parties that fail to perform this task provide executives with greater opportunities to abuse their power. *Well-functioning
political parties, therefore, are of utmost importance not only to democratic governance in general but also quite likely to robust economic performance in particular as well.* But such parties may take time to build;
they will not spring up overnight. Again, we emphasize that this is the
sort of finding that both democracy promoters and those concerned with
economic growth in the aid community should find relevant to their
respective agendas.

Democratic Institutions and Economic Policy

It is not just the electoral process and the composition of political parties (both governing and in opposition) that can shape economic policy and performance in democratic states, contributing to (or undermining) the eventual consolidation of democratic regimes. The structure of
democratic institutions also plays a crucial role, and many scholars of
young democracies in particular would argue that whether a country
is presidential or parliamentary will play a large role in shaping both
its economy and its subsequent chances of survival. Specifically, young

democracies that establish presidential regimes are said to face particularly grave risks of abuses of executive power, given the weakness of other institutions that have likely been crippled by earlier authoritarian (especially military) rulers (Cheibub 2006). One can name any number of leaders in recent years (e.g., Hugo Chavez in Venezuela and Vladimir Putin in Russia) who have sought to increase executive power at the expense of other institutional arrangements.

We acknowledge that institutional arrangements come, of course, in many varieties and that our distinction between presidential and parliamentary regimes will strike many scholars as overly simplistic. Russia in 2007, for example, had a strong president in Vladimir Putin (alongside a weak prime minister), but following presidential elections in 2008 it seemed increasingly likely that Putin would become a strong prime minister (alongside a relatively weak president). Still, because much of the relevant literature has been based on this fundamental division, including with respect to the consequences for economic policy, we rely on it for our purposes here as well.

In this section, we examine how the distribution of power between the executive, legislative, and judicial branches of government can influence a country's trajectory. We first turn our attention to the two main variants of democratic organization, namely presidentialism and parliamentarism, before turning our attention to the division of power between the elected branches of government and unelected institutions, including the judiciary and central bank.

The rationale for drawing the distinction between presidential and parliamentary regimes in terms of their effects on economic policy and democratic consolidation is as follows. In theory, presidential regimes are characterized by a separation of powers of the kind that America's founding fathers sought to engineer in the Constitution between the U.S. president and the Congress.[8] This system of "checks and balances" ideally prevents elected officials, in particular the executive, from

---

[8] Federalist Paper 51 presents the rationale behind the separation of powers enshrined in the U.S. Constitution.

abusing their powers because other branches of government serve a watchdog function. In an important sense, checks and balances provide the institutional correlate to contested elections: they both act to discipline politicians.[9]

At the same time, there is a price to be paid for this splintering of political power in that divided government creates the potential for gridlock should the president and the legislature fail to agree. Additionally, some scholars have argued that presidential democracies will find it difficult to generate public goods, with spending instead targeted by politicians at their preferred, winning coalition of interest groups. Because the president cannot hope to build a "big tent" that incorporates all the factions that will inevitably sit in opposition, she will simply focus on building a winning coalition in the legislature and shower that group with the goods and the rents they seek from government.

Under a (Westminster) parliamentary system, in contrast, the party in power controls the government and its policies. Although there are benefits associated with this system – governments have a better chance of executing the policies they adopt – there are costs as well. The resulting economic policies, for example, may be developed and carried out with little public debate, and this could lead to poor performance that undermines democratic stability.

Fractured parliamentary systems, in which multiple parties must form a coalition, face a different set of challenges. Given these circumstances, efforts to achieve a majority may prove unstable or the resulting government may prove unable to develop consistent policies, with detrimental effects on the economy (Bernhard, Reenock, and Nordstrom, 2001). Nonetheless, during the third wave of democratization, many academics and policy-makers have encouraged new democracies to adopt multiparty, parliamentary forms of government. According to

---

[9] For example, James Madison notes in Federalist Paper 51 that because leaders are subject to elections and face a division of powers among the branches of government, "a double security arises to the rights of the people."

this argument, because many past ills have stemmed from unaccountable presidents circumventing or ignoring the legislature, a parliamentary system, in which the executive holds power only as long as she can maintain majority support in the legislature, is best suited to prevent abuses of power.

However, it remains unclear which regime type – parliamentary or presidential – generates higher levels of long-run growth, particularly in young democracies. Many scholars would argue that the evidence points in favor of parliamentary regimes, asserting that in developing countries presidents tend to be strong and abusive of their powers, whereas legislatures are weak and fail to provide the checks and balances function (Persson and Tabellini 2003). Furthermore, parliamentary systems, particularly of the Westminster variety, may prove more stable in the face of severe economic challenges, when democratic governments are weakest and most likely to be reversed.

In an important article, Bernhard, Reenock and Nordstrom (2001) compared the durability of different sorts of democratic institutional structures in the face of economic downturns. They find evidence that those parliamentary systems that do not have high levels of party fragmentation (e.g., Westminster democracies) fare better than other regime types under conditions of crisis because their ability to concentrate power allows them to rapidly formulate coherent policy responses. In contrast, "Under conditions of economic crisis, pluralist systems [presidential systems or those with a proliferation of parties], with their propensity to disperse power, are much more likely to deadlock, making them more prone to break down. Their ability to formulate responses to crises is more limited because of the necessity of formulating a consensus or compromise between the legislative and executive branches" (Bernhard, Reenock and Nordstrom 2001, 781–782).

In the following chapter we will devote significant attention to the relationship between presidential versus parliamentary systems and economic performance and the consequences for democratic consolidation and reversal. As we will see, our findings differ in important respects from the literature just cited, and we will claim that what is most essential for democratic consolidation is the extent to which states have developed *effective* checks and balances on the executive, no matter whether she is a president or a prime minister. We note here, however, that one reason for the difference between our findings as opposed to that of scholars like Bernhard, Reenock and Nordstrom stems from the fact that we are using a complete data set of the world's young democracies since 1960, whereas other findings were based on data that either combined both the industrial and developing worlds or were incomplete (many data sets, for example, exclude short-lived periods of democracy or do not incorporate the post-Soviet bloc nations).

Nearly as important for economic policy and performance as the allocation of power between the executive and legislative branches is the separation between these elected branches and unelected bodies, such as the judiciary, the central bank, and the bureaucracy. Traditionally, the focus in this area has been on the judiciary, as the central bank and the bureaucracy are in theory divisions within the executive branch, but recent work has come to view the independence of all three as crucial to overall institutional quality. Of course, the practical degree of insulation that courts, central banks, and treasury authorities have from democratic politics is open to debate in every country, though it is clear that there is a large degree of variation among them in their independence.

The extent to which democracy, generally speaking, improves the quality of judicial and monetary institutions among others has lately been the subject of much debate and research. This debate is significant because organizations like the World Bank now routinely assert that "good governance" is essential for economic growth, without explicitly stating that democracy is generally required for achieving good governance in the first place. Rivera-Batiz (2002), for example, finds that greater democracy is associated with higher institutional quality. Additional support for the positive relationship between democracy and institutional quality comes from Rigobon and Rodrik (2004), who find that greater democratic freedom and better respect for the rule of law are mutually reinforcing. Also supporting the contention that democracy bolsters institutional quality are findings by Beck and Laeven (2005) in a study of economic performance in post-communist countries. They find that the level of constraints on the executive in 1992, for example, is significantly and positively associated with the level of institutional development in 1996.

Focusing on monetary policy as a case study, Keefer and Stasavage (2003) find that democratic institutions generally enhance the quality of decision-making. They note that monetary policy credibility depends crucially not simply on factors like central bank independence but also on the extent of checks and balances in place among government institutions to guarantee central bank independence. Formal structures such as constitutionally established vetoes can help to put such checks in place but so can multiparty democracy in which policy can be enacted only after reaching an accord with opposition parties or groups (this finding is also supported with case study evidence in Guillaume and Stasavage 1999) . In fact, where party competition is absent, formal or constitutional checks may have little practical influence over government decision-making. This is a concern, for example, in contemporary South Africa, where politics are dominated by the African National Congress.

But under what conditions are "founding fathers" (and "mothers") motivated to produce "better" institutions that deliver something approximating "good governance"? In other words, if we reject initial conditions determinism, where do the motivations come from that induce leaders to develop institutions and policies that serve the general welfare? *It is clear that understanding the precise causal mechanisms that produce better institutions in democratic settings is a major research challenge.* Among the many variables that may influence institutional performance, one that is receiving renewed attention is *time*. Simply stated, older democracies seem to perform better than younger ones, in part because institutions have had time to mature and to become credible. We discuss in greater detail in the next section how the age of a democracy might influence its economic policy and performance and its chances for consolidation.

Does Age Matter?

One of the major findings of the vast literature on democratic consolidation is that the older a democracy is, the less likely it is to fail. Thus, the time in which a country has experienced democracy, or what is called its "stock" of democracy, seems to matter to regime survival (Gerring et al. 2005). We will examine that finding empirically in the following chapter; here we look at the theory.

Interestingly, time was not always viewed by scholars or even practitioners as a crucial variable in determining how a young democracy might fare. Jose Maria Maravall – who is among those rare individuals who have worked both as a senior politician and as a leading academic – has, for example, written that "There is no evidence...that the passage of time itself can substantially modify a given political culture..." (Maravall 1995, 25).

With all due respect to Maravall, however, recent scholarship has demonstrated that the length of a given democratization episode may be crucial to democratic consolidation, precisely because it allows the space in which the widely held "culture" or view within a given society that democracy is the best political regime for peacefully reconciling divergent views and interests about politics and economics can emerge. It also enables countries to develop the human capital needed to support democracy (i.e., an educated population) – which can take many years – while also enabling political institutions, like parties, to mature and cohere. Thus, democracy may be usefully conceptualized as a "stock" variable whose positive effects are only felt over time; more on this in the following chapter (Gerring et al. 2005; Persson and Tabellini 2006).

Young democracies face a high degree of uncertainty in two key areas that make them particularly fragile in their early years. First, political actors may be unsure about each others' commitment to maintaining the nascent democratic regime. Electoral processes, the composition of political parties, and institutional mandates may all be fluid and heavily contested in the immediate period following democratization and perhaps for several years thereafter. These conditions can produce a shortening of time horizons, as politicians act to stave off any immediate threat to the democratic order or to secure their institutional mandates, resulting in policies that may dampen medium- and long-term prospects for both economic and democratic development (Haggard and Kaufman 1995, 152).

Second, and as already discussed, voters in a new democracy may doubt the credibility of politicians' promises, and politicians, in turn, may doubt whether voters will lend their electoral support in response to campaign promises (Keefer 2007a). This problem is exacerbated where an active, free press that informs voters with respect to the performance of their politicians is lacking and where the educational system has been weak.

In this setting, politicians and voters in new democracies may circumvent the resulting political market failures by relying on existing patronage networks – for example, ethnic, religious, or geographical groups – which can ensure that voters turn out at the polls and that politicians deliver on their targeted promises. The big city political machines run by bosses in the United States in the late nineteenth and early twentieth centuries constitute one example of such networks, and a key aspect of the machine system was the participation of recent immigrants for whom the U.S. democratic system was new. Ethnically based political parties in sub-Saharan Africa provide another example of this phenomenon. Keefer (2007b) tests this argument empirically and finds that longer periods of democracy are associated with lower corruption, higher bureaucratic quality, and the rule of law.

New democracies may also face particular difficulties in adopting optimal economic policies, over and above the challenges discussed in the previous sections of this chapter. As Haggard and Kaufman stress, "new democratic governments face exceptionally strong distributive pressures, both from groups re-entering the political arena after long periods of repression and from established interests demanding reassurance. Uncertainties with respect to the stability of the new democratic order, moreover, affect the time horizons of both private and public actors" and result in policies – or their absence – that could dampen medium- and long-term prospects for both economic and democratic development (Haggard and Kaufman 1995, 152).

However, not all theorists have seen young democracies as being particularly ill prepared for the task of enacting reforms. Olson's (1982) analysis, discussed in the first section of this chapter, suggests that early on, before interest groups have become entrenched and have secured control over policy, may be the best (indeed *only*) time in which to undertake a policy shift. As we discuss in the next chapter, our data analysis as well as a number of recent studies support this view; anecdotally, one need only look at the difficulties that Western European countries have had in enacting economic reforms to see that young democracies may face different, but not necessarily higher, barriers to policy change.[10]

Even if the leaders of a young democracy show a willingness to pursue economic reforms, domestic challenges will likely persist. As Joan Nelson points out, "Many countries have launched promising reform efforts; far fewer have sustained those efforts long and vigorously enough to produce results. The toughest political challenges often come *after* the initial reforms have been launched" (Nelson 1995, 49). As has been widely discussed in the literature on the political economy of economic reform, benefits from reform frequently take time to materialize, as in the former communist countries where the immediate effects of liberalization measures included spikes in inflation and unemployment and sharp contractions in output. Furthermore, "the economic reform agenda changes significantly between the launch phase and later phases. The character of politics . . . also tends to change" (Nelson 1995, 47). This analysis underlines the need to provide sustained support to the world's

---

[10] We thank Karen Remmer for this very useful comparison.

young democratizers at an early stage in their development (more on this issue later).

We would also note that the extent to which the economic benefits of democracy take time to materialize acquires particular importance due to the economic circumstances that many new democracies inherit. Around the world, many new democracies emerge in the face of difficult economic conditions. Elected leaders take office in the immediate aftermath of economic crisis (as in Indonesia, where the collapse of the Suharto regime occurred during the Asian financial crisis of 1997–1998), in conflict settings (e.g., Afghanistan and Iraq), during periods when commodity prices are falling (as in several African states), or following the collapse of an entire political-economic system (as in the post-communist transition economies). They are therefore immediately faced with the twin challenges – the "dual transition" – of shoring up their fragile democracies while placing their economies on a path that generates employment and income growth (Centeno 1994).

But postponing economic reform until well-functioning democratic institutions take root and consolidate is often simply not an option for governments that, for example, desperately need assistance from the International Monetary Fund and/or from foreign investors, both direct and portfolio. In these cases, both lenders and investors will require assurances that governments have set a path toward economic stabilization.

The age of democracy and its relationship to economic policy and performance is a crucial issue from a policy-making standpoint because most democracies that collapse do so within their first five years of existence. This implies that the foreign assistance community needs to pay particular attention to democracies during their early years and provide the support needed to help them consolidate, a lesson that seems especially pertinent today as the United States and other nations struggle to consolidate democracy in such "postconflict" environments as Afghanistan or where democracy is fragile, as in Haiti. Aid might be among the foreign policies that can help consolidate young democracies, but other growth-enhancing policies – like openness to trade from these states – will need to be considered as well, not to mention the provision of security, without which political and economic development are near impossible. We discuss these issues in greater detail in the final two chapters of this book.

Conclusions

As a political system with a distinctive set of processes (e.g., competitive elections) and institutions (e.g., multiparty legislatures), democracies have a number of attributes that have been posited by scholars to have important economic effects, not all of which are deemed to be conducive to growth. As we have seen, scholars remain divided on whether democracy is, on balance, a positive or a negative for long-run economic performance, and regression analysis – including those we have performed with our own data set (see the following chapter) – has yet to prove the case one way or the other. In fact, we believe that "democracy" might be too coarse a variable to be policy relevant (much less analytically useful) and that the *type* of democracy matters greatly as well.

By way of summary, we have found that elections and political institutions hold the promise of improving a country's economic performance by disciplining politicians but only under certain conditions. When countries are deeply divided, when politicians lack credibility, and when governments and institutions lack legitimacy, it will prove difficult to articulate much less advance the sorts of economic policies that promote democratic consolidation. In short, when *political arrangements encourage politicians to concentrate power, or induce them to target specific groups at the expense of broader social welfare, then democracy is less likely to take root.* In the next chapter we test this proposition using descriptive statistics and regression analysis.

2 Why Do Young Democracies Fail?

New democracies are, in effect, in a catch-22 situation: lacking legitimacy they cannot become effective; lacking effectiveness they cannot develop legitimacy.

Samuel P. Huntington (1991, 258)

N THIS CHAPTER WE EXPLORE THE FACTORS THAT SEEM TO increase the risk that a young democracy will be overthrown. The first section of the chapter opens by presenting descriptive statistics comparing failed democracies to those that have endured through 2004, the end of our sample period. Although more recent cases of democratic reversal, such as Thailand, Fiji, and Russia, are not included in our data set, we discuss them here and in other chapters. We then go on to make use of hazard model regressions to ascertain which of the many variables we highlight in this overview are most strongly associated with the reversal of democracy.

We note that although much of the earlier academic work that relates institutions, economic performance, and democratic survival (which we review later) has sought to discern causal connections between such broad variables as "democracy" on the one hand and "growth" on the other, our specific purpose here is to present a more nuanced account of the relationships between democratic institutions and a number of policy variables and outcomes. This is essential because some of the more aggregate-level work may lead us, like the fabled drunk, to search for the key to understanding democratic survival under the lamppost even if we need to look elsewhere. It is plausible, for example, that the best hopes for a young democracy are not immediately related to its growth performance but rather to its success at sharing the wealth through redistributive measures. Nonetheless, much of the prior work on democratic survival and reversal has focused on growth as *the* crucial variable. In short, it is our contention that unpacking both democracy and growth is crucial for policy-relevant analysis.

As mentioned, we base our analysis on a data set of democratizations that occurred between 1960 and 2004. We built this data set using the widely used Polity IV democracy measures, in conjunction with several other public sources of economic and political data (see the appendices for more details on our methodology and data set). In particular, rather than simply setting an arbitrary threshold Polity score as constituting a shift to a democracy, we coded as a democratization episode any positive change of 6 or more points in a country's Polity score in a given year. Although theoretically this methodology could classify as a democratizer a country which had a very low score even after such a change, this did not happen in practice. Still, given this approach, the term *democratizers* rather than *democracies* might be a more precise description of the countries in our data set. Conversely, we classify periods of democratic governance as having ended when the Polity score drops more than 6 points; again, while in theory a country could suffer such a loss and remain nominally democratic, there are no such cases in practice. In what follows, we refer to returns to authoritarianism as democratic reversals or simply reversals.

This methodology identified 123 democratization episodes in 88 countries between 1960 and 2004 (a list of the democratizations included in our data set can be found in Appendix 2). Of these democratizations, 26 took place in Latin America, four were in Western Europe, 21 in Eastern Europe, 46 in sub-Saharan Africa, three in the Middle East and North Africa region, and 23 in Asia. Table 2.1 makes clear the importance of regional trends in the timing of democratizations, with sub-Saharan

TABLE 2.1. *Democratizations by region and decade*

	1960s	1970s	1980s	1990s	After 2000	Total
Total	<u>26</u>	<u>20</u>	<u>17</u>	<u>52</u>	<u>8</u>	<u>123</u>
Latin America	6	3	11	5	1	26
Western Europe	1	3	0	0	0	4
Eastern Europe	0	0	0	19	2	21
Sub-Saharan Africa	15	6	2	19	4	46
Middle East-N. Africa	0	1	1	1	0	3
Asia	4	7	3	8	1	23

Source: Polity IV, author's calculations.

African countries – mainly those gaining independence – making up the majority of democratizations in the 1960s and 1970s. By contrast, 11 of 17 democratizations in the 1980s took place in Latin America, and over 70 percent of democratizations in the 1990s occurred in Eastern Europe and sub-Saharan Africa.

Democratic Survival and Reversal

We now turn our attention to the factors that seem to promote democratic survival – or lead to reversal – in our sample of new democracies. We first use descriptive statistics to guide us with respect to whether differences can be discerned among those states that successfully consolidate their democracies (meaning that they survive) and those that reverse. As we will see, some intriguing differences do indeed emerge. We subsequently employ regression analysis to assess the *relative importance* of the various bivariate relationships that we discover.

Of the 123 democratic regimes created in our data set, 67 survived through 2004, the end of our sample period, while 56 had been reversed. As is evident in Table 2.2, rates of reversal vary widely among regions. Although sub-Saharan Africa has been the site of nearly twice as many democratizations as any other region, 63 percent of African democratizations ended in reversal (see Table 2.2). Latin American and Asian democratizers have also exhibited limited durability, with nearly

TABLE 2.2. *Democratizations by region and outcome*

	Sustained	Reversed
Total	<u>67</u>	<u>56</u>
Latin America	17	9
Western Europe	3	1
Eastern Europe	19	2
Sub-Saharan Africa	17	29
Middle East-N. Africa	1	2
Asia	10	13

Source: Polity IV, author's calculations.

35 percent and 57 percent, respectively, undergoing reversal. By contrast, over 90 percent of Eastern European democratizations had been sustained as of 2004. North Africa and the Middle East have seen few democratizations, sustained or otherwise.[1] The significance of these regional variations is discussed later in this chapter, while Chapter 4 explores the factors behind this variation.

Of those cases that ended in a reversal, the average length of the democratic episode was just under six years. Almost 68 percent of unsuccessful democratizations ended during the first five years and nearly 84 percent of unsuccessful democratizations failed within the first 10 years (see Figure 2.1). Indeed, roughly one-quarter of all new democracies since 1960 failed within the first two years.

Figure 2.2 makes clear that this decline in vulnerability over time is not merely a product of attrition bias, as the *rate* at which democracies are reversed declines over time.[2] This distribution, which has been

---

[1] In the post-1960 period, Turkey had one democratization that was reversed and another that was sustained. Reforms in Iran in the late 1990s resulted in its being qualified as a democratizer in 1997, but a rollback of these reforms in 2003 meant that this democratization was classified as having been reversed. Between 1997 and 2003, Polity assigned Iran a score of three, a ranking also applied to South Korea in the late 1960s and Malaysia since 1995. In 2004, Iran's Polity score fell to −6.

[2] Specifically, this is the number of young democracies that reverse each year, divided by the total number of young democracies at the beginning of each year. Other authors have called this the "breakdown rate" (Bernhard, Reenock, and Nordstrom 2001, 2003).

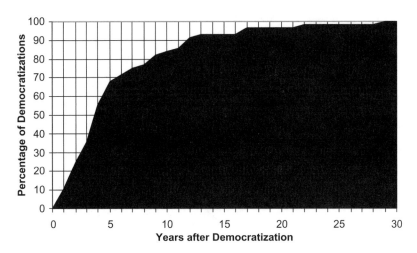

FIGURE 2.1. Democratic Reversals: Cumulative Percentage Distribution. *Source:* Polity IV, authors' calculations.

noted by other authors as well (Bernhard, Reenock, and Nordstrom 2003; Gasiorowski and Power 1998), drives our contention that democratic regimes are particularly vulnerable in their early years. Although it is important to note that we find no threshold age beyond which a

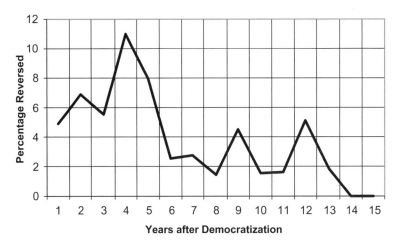

FIGURE 2.2. Rates of Democratic Reversal over Time. *Source:* Polity IV, authors' calculations.

TABLE 2.3. *Repeated attempts at democratization*

	Sustained	Reversed
Total	<u>67</u>	<u>56</u>
First Democratization	29	33
Second Democratization	26	15
Third Democratization	7	5
Fourth Democratization	4	2
Fifth Democratization[a]	0	1
Sixth Democratization[a]	1	0

[a] Only Peru underwent more than four democratizations.
Source: Polity IV, authors' calculations.

democratic government is apparently safe from overthrow (again think of Thailand, which reversed in 2006 after 14 years of democracy), we therefore focus mainly on the first five years of democracy in our analysis of the factors associated with the success and failure of democratic regimes.

Among those democracies that were reversed, several then later underwent second and even third democratization episodes. As Table 2.3 indicates, the chances that democracy was sustained increased with each successive attempt. Whereas only around 47 percent of cases in which countries underwent democratization for the first time were sustained, those undergoing democratization for the second time succeeded almost 64 percent of the time, and four of the six cases in which countries made a fourth attempt at democratic governance were sustained as of 2004. Only Peru and Pakistan failed to sustain their fourth democratization, and Peru was the sole country to have undergone more than four democratizations.[3]

---

[3] Although events in Thailand during 2006 presumably constituted a reversal of that country's fourth attempt at democracy, our data set ends in 2004, and so this is not included in our analysis. Other likely reversals that occurred after the end of our data set include events in Russia, East Timor, Fiji, and Bangladesh.

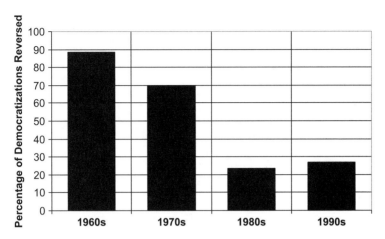

FIGURE 2.3. Reversal Rates by Decade. *Source:* Polity IV, authors' calculations.

This trend is closely aligned with the improving success rate of democratizations over time, as is clear from Figure 2.3. Only 11.5 percent of the democratizations in the 1960s were sustained, whereas 30 percent of those taking place in the 1970s were sustained. The success rate reached 76.5 percent in the 1980s and 73 percent in the 1990s. This change in success rates over time has not yet been explained, to the best of our knowledge. Here we quickly mention some possible explanations that we considered, while leaving further analysis to the concluding chapter.

First, one could argue that democracies that came into existence later have simply had less time to run into difficulty. If this were the case, then we would expect that the reversal rate of democracies of any given age would not differ significantly. However, rates of reversal were significantly higher in the pre-1980 period in democracies of almost every age, as is evident in Figure 2.4.

Second, one might suggest that first attempts at democratization in African and Asian countries following independence in the 1960s and 1970s ran into trouble because of the dislocations caused by

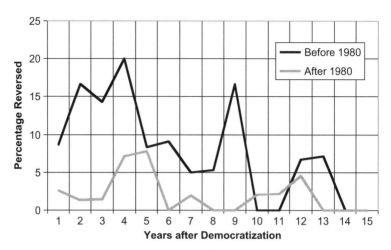

FIGURE 2.4. Reversal Rates Before and After 1980. *Source:* Polity IV, authors' calculations.

decolonization. However, the success rate for democratization improved in all countries, not only those that had recently gained their independence in the 1960s and 1970s.

Third, one might hypothesize that the spike in success rates was skewed by the relative success of democracy in the post-communist states of Eastern Europe and the former Soviet Union. Democratizations that took place in other regions outside the former Soviet bloc, however, were also more likely to be sustained if they took place after 1980.

Fourth, one could suggest that global support for democracy has increased over time. Figure 2.5 demonstrates that although foreign aid to young democracies was actually lower during the 1980s, it did in fact increase substantially in the 1990s and after (see Finkel, Perez-Linan, and Seligson 2006). Thus, it is plausible that greater backing from the international community may be the source of the improvement. Relatedly, regional and international institutions like the European Union, North American Free Trade Area, and World Trade Organization could serve to help "lock-in" democratic reforms (see Pevehouse 2002; Mansfield and Pevehouse 2006).

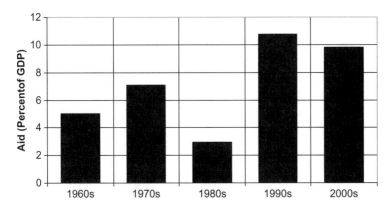

FIGURE 2.5 Average Aid during First 5 Years of Democracy. *Source:* Polity IV, WDI, authors' calculations.

Finally, the process of globalization might support young democracies through a variety of pathways reported in the political economy literature (on trade and democracy see Lopez-Cordova and Meissner 2005). Acemoglu and Robinson (2006), for example, have highlighted the increasing ease of capital flight in supporting the democratization process. This is because as capital becomes more mobile, the wealthy are satisfied that their assets are safe against possible seizure by the potentially revolutionary poor. Knowing that they cannot seize the assets of the rich, the poor then settle for democracy and the franchise as a compromise that, if nothing more, is likely to win them at least some election-induced redistribution. Yet, as compelling as this model might be, it would seem that the rich have always been able to move their money in times of trouble, and if their main asset is in land, then globalization would be of little help to them (Acemoglu and Robinson 2006; Eichengreen and Leblang 2006).

Overall, then, we have been unable to determine (nor are we aware of any work that has succeeded in so doing) what exactly changed in the late 1970s that made subsequent democratizations more likely to succeed, and we see this as a crucial area for further research.

TABLE 2.4. *Initial conditions and democratic reversals*

| | Averages, first five years | | Difference |
	Reversed	Sustained	(p-value)
Per Capita Income[a]	866	2,617	1,750
(Std. Dev.)	(1209.2)	(2954.5)	(0.00)
Gini Coefficient	47.1	42.8	4.3
(Std. Dev.)	(3.8)	(7.2)	(0.00)
Poverty Rate ($1/day)	37.1	17.1	20.0
(Std. Dev.)	(27.6)	(21.1)	(0.01)
Infant Mortality[b]	110.7	55.2	55.4
(Std. Dev.)	(45.7)	(38.5)	(0.00)
Ethnic Fragmentation	0.55	0.45	0.10
(Std. Dev.)	(0.29)	(0.24)	(0.02)

[a] 2006 dollars.
[b] Per 1,000 live births.
Source: WDI, UTIP, Alesina et al. (2003), Polity IV, authors' calculations.

Descriptive Statistics

We now turn to some features of young democracies that are frequently cited as possible causes of variation in their economic performance and political development. Table 2.4 compares average initial conditions (during the first five years of the democratic regime or the duration of the regime if it lasted less than five years) in democracies that were reversed with the conditions in democracies that were sustained through 2004. Sustained democratizations have tended to occur in relatively wealthier countries, with an average income of $2,618 (2006 dollars), compared with an average of around $866 for young democracies that end in reversal. Our updated data set confirms the finding of Przeworski et al. (2000) that the probability that democracy is reversed once income tops $4,000 approaches zero, although it is worth recalling that there are outliers in the data, in that Argentina experienced a democratic reversal in 1976, despite lying well above the $4,000 threshold.

Figures on per capita income, however, may conceal severe inequities within a given society, whether of income, assets, or opportunities, which may play a significant role in determining how a democracy fares and whether it ultimately consolidates and survives. If large segments of the population do not share in the nation's wealth, they may view the political order, even if "democratic" in institutional form, as being unresponsive or even detrimental to their interests.

Our data show that inequality was indeed significantly higher in democracies that eventually underwent a reversal. Likewise, the poverty rate (the percentage of the population living on less than one Purchasing Power Parity (PPP) adjusted dollar per day) is on average higher in countries in which democratization was reversed than in those where it was sustained, with an average of around 40 percent of the population living on less than one dollar per day in the former, as against just over 20 percent in the latter. Similarly, infant mortality provides an indicator of how broadly the benefits of economic growth have been distributed. The average rate of infant mortality per 1,000 live births during the first five years of democracy is fully twice as high in countries where democracy is reversed as in countries where democracy is sustained. *This stark difference suggests that the extent to which economic development has benefited all citizens may be a key factor in determining how democracy fares; economic growth alone may be insufficient to ensure democratic consolidation.*

Some noneconomic divisions in societies also appear to play a role in determining the fate of democracy. For example, ethnic fragmentation was significantly higher in those cases where democracy was reversed than where democratic governments persisted through the end of the period under study (see Table 2.4). Indeed, Figure 2.6 illustrates, democratizations in countries with ethnic fragmentation greater than the world average are reversed 51 percent of the time, as compared to 38 percent of the time when ethnic fragmentation was below average.[4]

---

[4] We recognize that ethnicity is a political construction rather than a "natural" initial condition such as geography, but for our purposes it seems fair to treat it as a condition that governments can do little to change, and may well seek to exploit, over their electoral time horizon.

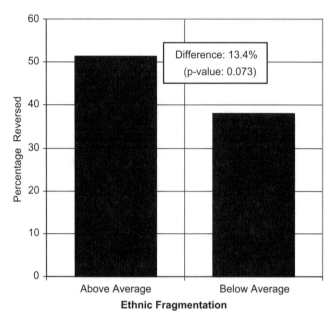

FIGURE 2.6. Ethnic Fragmentation and Democratic Reversals. *Source:* Alesina et al. (2003), Polity IV, authors' calculations.

This result is consistent with the work of Adsera and Boix (2004), who find that greater ethnic fragmentation is associated with instability in democracies.

To summarize, our preliminary examination of the data indicates that the initial conditions under which democratizations take place do exert a significant impact on the survival of the regime. Low per capita income, high levels of inequality, high rates of poverty, and higher ethnic fragmentation negatively impact the chance that democracy will be sustained. However, we wish to emphasize that these relationships are not deterministic. As Table 2.5 makes clear, there are several countries in which initial conditions were extremely unfavorable, yet democracy was sustained. Moreover, we wish to stress that most of the countries in our data set that reversed in the past have subsequently redemocratized, a fact that has seemingly escaped many advocates of "initial

TABLE 2.5. *"Hard Cases," democratizations in low-income, high-inequality, ethnically fragmented countries*

Country	Year of democratization	Year of reversal (if any)
Nigeria	1960	1963
Kenya	1963	1968
Zambia	1964	1971
Ecuador	1968	1969
Thailand	1969	1970
Ghana	1970	1971
Pakistan	1973	1976
Thailand	1974	1975
Thailand	1978	1990
Ghana	1979	1980
Uganda	1980	1984
Bolivia	1982	
Sudan	1986	1988
Pakistan	1988	1998
Nepal	1990	2001
Benin	1991	
Zambia	1991	
Ghana	1992	
Central African Republic	1993	2002
Mozambique	1994	
Malawi	1994	
Ethiopia	1995	
Sierra Leone	1996	1996
Nigeria	1999	
Indonesia	1999	
Senegal	2000	
Ivory Coast	2000	2001
Kenya	2002	

Source: WDI, UTIP, Alesina et al. (2003), Polity IV, authors' calculations.

conditions determinism." Consequently, the challenge for the researcher is to determine how democratic regimes have on many occasions persevered under trying circumstances.

The literature on the causes of democratic reversal has long emphasized that democracy is put under stress by poor economic performance. But looking just at the average growth rates in our data set, we see that

TABLE 2.6. *Economic performance and democratic reversals*

	Averages, first five years		Difference (p-value)
	Reversed	Sustained	
Growth	3.8	1.5	2.3
(Std. Dev.)	(4.80)	(5.94)	(0.01)
Investment	18.4	19.8	1.4
(Std. Dev.)	(8.78)	(6.38)	(0.16)
Inflation	167.3	161.0	6.3
(Std Dev.)	(782.50)	(496.50)	(0.48)
Median	10.824	18.205	

Source: WDI, Polity IV, authors' calculations.

those democratic regimes that were sustained averaged annual growth of only 1.5 percent, as compared to nearly 3.8 percent during the initial five years of democracies that were ultimately reversed (see Table 2.6). The reader might suspect that these findings are driven by the Eastern European cases in our sample, where democratization was accompanied by an economic collapse of Great Depression proportions. At the same time, we recall the recent example of Thailand, where economic growth did not seem to prevent reversal from occurring. Overall, these examples suggest the possibility that *low economic growth per se is not a clear sign that democracy is threatened and, conversely, that high economic growth is not a guarantee against democratic reversal.* We will have more to say about this, however, in the context of our regression analysis. To flag our general view, however, we remind readers that it may not be growth alone that is doing the work with respect to democratic survival or failure but other factors that need to be unpacked.

   In contrast to growth rates, we do find that rates of investment are significantly higher in sustained democracies than in countries where democracy is overthrown, which we believe is of great interest, though we do not pursue the underlying reasons here. It suggests that domestic investors might know something about their democracy's prospects from the very beginning of the democratization episode. Where democracy reversed, investment averaged around 18 percent, both in the five-year period before democratization and in the five-year period after democratization. Investment averaged around 20 percent in both periods in cases where democracy was sustained. Consequently, it appears that higher investment may signal overall more favorable conditions, both before and after democratization, as opposed to an improvement associated with the end of authoritarianism.

In our sample, inflation was somewhat more clearly related to democratic reversal than most other economic variables. Where democracy was ultimately reversed, inflation in the first five years of democracy had jumped relative to the five years prior in 74 percent of cases, and often increased sharply, while it remained on average unchanged in sustained democratizations, falling slightly in a majority of cases. This relationship may stem from the fact that inflation erodes real incomes in a manner that is very noticeable and very frustrating for a country's population. Interestingly, though, hyperinflation does not appear to be associated with the reversal of young democracies. Of the 20 young democracies in which the annual change in consumer prices topped 100 percent during the first five years, only five were reversed. This 25 percent reversal rate compares to a 43 percent reversal rate in young democracies where inflation remained under 100 percent during the early years.

As noted, since the early 1980s, the extent to which economic reforms and democratic consolidation are compatible has been a key question for economists and political scientists studying developing countries. Some have argued that the two processes are complimentary, but a more nuanced view is that this is the case so long as the sequencing and timing of the reform process is undertaken with political sensitivity.

Perhaps the strongest argument linking democratic consolidation with *gradual* economic reform, as opposed to "shock therapy," is found in Przeworski's and colleagues' insistence on the need for political legitimacy if the reform process is to advance in the face of political contestation (Bresser Pereira, Maravall, and Przeworski 1993). Rather than

operate by "speed and stealth," as some economists have urged the leaders of young democracies to do in order to take advantage of the "win-
dow of opportunity" available to them in promoting the reform process,
they argue that, to the contrary, reforms must be carried out in an open
and transparent fashion, one that takes seriously the concerns of the
wide range of social actors (Bresser Pereira, Maravall, and Przeworski
1993). That may slow the process, but it provides a more durable foundation for long-run economic growth. At the same time, Przeworski has
observed that this process may not be successful: "reforms can advance
quite far under democratic conditions, but they are politically destabilizing" (Przeworski 1991).

    Others have maintained that rapidly executed reforms carried out as
shock therapy actually benefit democratic development. The argument
for the shock therapy approach is that democracy and economic reform
are actually mutually reinforcing processes. As Steven Fish writes based
on the Eastern European experience, "economic reform is...closely
and positively related to democratization....Rapid liberalization helps
to pluralize economic power, thereby creating a firmer financial basis
for the emergence and development of non-state organizations that can
check the growth of executive absolutism" (Fish 2001, 82). In those instances where economic reform has been derailed, it has not been to the
benefit of democracy but rather has reflected the corruption of the process, in which "insiders" have seized both economic and political power.
Delay therefore does not benefit the median voter or the interests of
workers fearful of change but rather only works to the benefit of those
who benefit from partial reforms to their personal advantage (Hellman
1998).

    We will examine whether democracy impedes economic reform later
in this chapter. Here, we simply note that trade as a percentage of
gross domestic product (GDP) increased following democratization in
over 60 percent of cases, both in the subgroup of young democracies
that were ultimately reversed and in those that were sustained. Indeed,

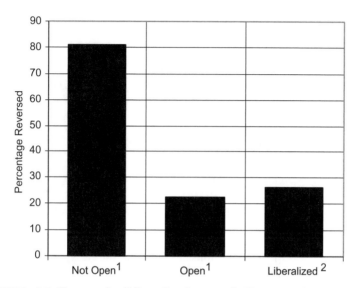

FIGURE 2.7. Economic Liberalization and Democratic Reversals.
(1) During entire the democratic episode; (2) At some point during
the democratic episode. *Source:* Wacziarg and Horn Welch (2003),
Polity IV, authors' calculations.

Figure 2.7 indicates that those democracies in which the economy
remained closed according to the well-known Sachs–Warner criteria
were overthrown at a rate nearly four times greater than that of democracies that undertook economic liberalization (as indicated by a shift in
the country's Sachs–Warner openness score from zero to one). Clearly,
increased trade does not automatically prompt resentment that sets back
democracy and, as we will discuss later, neither does democracy make
expanding trade impossible.

As we mentioned in the introduction and the previous chapter, the
literature on democratic political institutions has most frequently compared parliamentary and presidential systems, generally finding the former to be more durable than the latter (Przeworski et al. 2000), at least
under certain circumstances (Bernhard, Reenock, and Nordstrom 2001).
The results from our data set differ notably from the findings of this

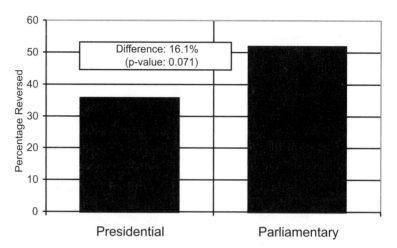

FIGURE 2.8. Political Institutions and Democratic Reversal. *Source:* WB DPI, Przeworski et al. (2000), Polity IV, authors' calculations.

earlier work. Of the 123 democratizations between 1960 and 2004, 81 initially put in place presidential systems and 27 put in place parliamentary systems (data were not available on the remaining 15 cases). Of the presidential systems, nearly 36 percent ended in reversal; just over one-half of the parliamentary regimes ended in reversal (Figure 2.8).

Strikingly, these ratios are almost the exact reverse of those recorded by Przeworski et al. (2000) in their seminal work. The difference in findings stems from two sources. First, and most simply, by looking only at countries that democratized after 1960, we are excluding a large number of European nations with parliamentary systems that were established much earlier.[5] Second, the difference is a result of the different methodologies used to classify governments as democratic or authoritarian. In particular, the emphasis that Przeworski et al. (2000) place on *alternation* of elected governments leads them to classify as authoritarian a number of governments that the Polity IV data lead us to

---

[5] This also helps to account for the difference between our data and that of Bernhard, Reenock, and Nordstrom (2001).

characterize as democratic.[6] Many of these are post-colonial cases in which a government came to power democratically, but never handed power to a democratically elected successor government. Thus, numerous short-lived experiments with parliamentary democracy are excluded from Przeworski et al.'s (2000) list of democracies. We believe that inclusion of these failed democracies in our study is justified, given that one of the threats that looms particularly large in new democracies is that the first duly elected government will refuse to hand over power to a successor, or alter the rules to prevent effective challenges.

As discussed earlier, parliamentary systems have been viewed as a tool to guard against abuses of executive power. Our data suggest that they have not performed this function particularly well in new democracies. Presumably, the institutional arrangement is not always enough to compensate for a lack of strong opposition parties and other effective checks and balances on the exercise of state power.

Consequently, we now turn our attention to the direct measure of constraints on executive power included in the Polity IV data set. Although the Polity data measures these limits on a scale from one (*"unlimited authority"*) to seven (*"executive parity or subordination"*) (Marshall and Jaggers 2005), we divide our 123 cases into two groups: those with a high level of executive constraints and those with a low level of executive constraints.[7] While the executive constraints score is indeed a component of the Polity score, the reader will recall that our definitions

---

[6] Whether alternation is a necessary condition for democracy is a key question in several high-profile cases. Is South Africa a democracy even if it has had only one party, the African National Congress (ANC), in power? Is Japan a democracy even though the Liberal Democratic Party (LDP) has dominated political life for 60 years? These questions are still debated by democracy scholars.

[7] For a democracy to be classified as having strong constraints on the executive, at a minimum other branches of government must be able to defeat executive proposals for action. The reader may object that the higher reversal rate simple reflects the fact that the government is more authoritarian to begin with, but as we make clear in Appendix 1, we define democratization and reversal not based on a *threshold* Polity score but rather in terms of the magnitude of a *change* in that score.

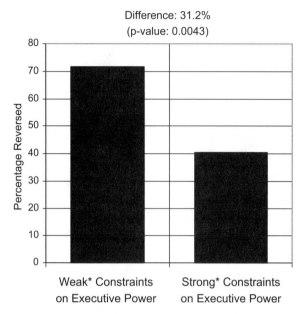

FIGURE 2.9. Constraints on Executive Power and Democratic Reversal.
*"Weak" constraints received a score less than 5 on Polity IV's scale of executive constraints. *Source:* Polity IV, authors' calculations.

of democratization and reversal refer to the magnitude of *changes* in the Polity score, as opposed to the *level* of that score.

This institutional feature does appear to have a significant relationship with the fate of the regime, as we see in Figure 2.9. In cases where these constraints on the executive are weak, democracy is reversed just over 70 percent of the time. By contrast, when constraints on the executive are strong, democracy is reversed only 40 percent of the time. *We therefore stress the importance of assessing the actual balance of power in new democracies; inferring that balance based on formal institutional structures may conceal a potential threat to democracy.* We thus echo David Hume, who wrote "...a republican and free government would be an obvious absurdity if the particular checks and controls provided by the constitution had really no influence and made it not the interest, even of bad men, to act for the public interest" (cited in Bueno de Mesquita et al. 2003, 18.) We will see in the following whether this finding is supported by our regression analysis.

Regression Analysis

In the previous section we examined a number of bivariate relationships between reversals in young democracies on the one hand and initial conditions, economic performance, economic reform, and political institutions on the other. However, we have not yet assessed the *relative* importance of these various factors for the survival of democracy. We now put our descriptive statistics into some context by presenting a series of multivariate regressions that show which factors are most strongly associated with an increased risk that the democracies in our sample will be overthrown. As discussed previously, our data set contains 123 cases of democratization from 1960 to 2004, with the shortest episode of democratic governance lasting one year and the longest lasting 43 years. This sample yields a total of 1,376 country-years of democracy during the period.

As a robustness check, we also ran the regressions presented here on a data set created using an alternate definition of democracy. Defining democracy as having a strictly positive Polity score (a methodology employed by Persson and Tabellini 2006, among others) identifies 136 democratizations in the period from 1960 to 2004. The results from this alternative data set, consisting of 1,481 country-years of democracy, were very similar to those from our own data set, with coefficient estimates close to those presented here and significance levels unchanged (these results are available from the authors on request).

Given the nature of our dependent variable, namely the risk of democratic reversal, it is appropriate to use event history methodology to analyze the data set we have built (for an excellent introduction see Box-Steffensmeier and Jones 2004). In particular, we employ a continuous time hazard model, which can deal with variables that vary from year to year, like inflation or economic growth. We used a Weibull model as opposed to, for example, an exponential model, because the descriptive statistics we examined in the previous section indicated that the rate of democratic reversal declined over time. The Weibull will allow us to explicitly test this hypothesis with the following model:

$$h(t \mid \mathbf{x}_t) = pt^{p-1} \exp(\beta_0 + \mathbf{x}_t\beta_1),$$

where $h(t \mid \mathbf{x}_t)$ is the (limiting or instantaneous) probability of democratic reversal and p is a time-dependence parameter. If the rate of democratic reversal is independent of the age of the democratic regime, p will be equal to one. The vector $\mathbf{x}$ contains independent variables selected based on the descriptive statistics we saw in the previous section. We also ran the regressions using an exponential model and a non-parametric Cox proportional hazard model. In both cases, the coefficient estimates and the results of significance tests were nearly identical to the results for the Weibull model that we present here.

The regressions results are summarized in Tables 2.7 to 2.9, which report the effect in percentage terms of a one-unit increase in each independent variable on the baseline hazard rate (the instantaneous risk of democratic reversal). For example, according to our estimates, a one-point increase in a country's Polity IV score for constraints on the executive reduces the risk of reversal by around 20 percent (when all other variables are set at zero).[8]

Table 2.7 presents the results on the relationship between economic performance and political institutions on the one hand and the risk of democratic reversal on the other, controlling for initial conditions using

---

[8] The exponential form of the model means that the marginal effects of each variable vary depending on the values taken by the other regressors.

Regressions: Impact on Risk of Democratic Failure, Weibull Hazard Model

Reporting estimated % change in baseline hazard rate resulting from a one-unit increase in the independent variable

	(1)	(2)	(3)	(4)	(5)	(6)	(7)	(8)	(9)
Growth	-0.072*** (0.022)								
Growth, 5-yr Ave		-0.114*** (0.029)				-0.075*** (0.028)	-0.072** (0.029)	-0.085*** (0.033)	-0.066** (0.031)
Log Inflation			1.343*** (0.330)			0.826*** (0.340)	0.834*** (0.320)	0.785*** (0.340)	0.883*** (0.380)
Investment				-0.050 (0.037)					
Investment, 5-yr Ave					-0.050 (0.032)				
Executive Constraints	-0.206 (0.110)	-0.223* (0.110)	-0.191 (0.110)	-0.201 (0.110)	-0.190 (0.110)	-0.214* (0.110)		-0.204* (0.110)	-0.225* (0.110)
Presidential							-0.097 (0.360)		
Prior Democratizations								0.227 (0.300)	
Cumulative Years of Democracy									-0.019 (0.013)
Log GDP per capita	-0.576*** (0.087)	-0.593*** (0.088)	-0.620*** (0.084)	-0.542*** (0.089)	-0.541*** (0.089)	-0.613*** (0.085)	-0.647*** (0.077)	-0.641*** (0.094)	-0.593*** (0.097)
Pre-1980	3.986*** (1.950)	5.366*** (2.540)	5.230*** (2.530)	3.752*** (1.840)	3.800*** (1.850)	5.857*** (2.770)	5.580*** (2.600)	6.075*** (2.860)	5.499*** (2.640)
Government Consumption (% GDP)	-0.105*** (0.038)	-0.110*** (0.037)	-0.105*** (0.036)	-0.095** (0.038)	-0.092* (0.037)	-0.110*** (0.037)	-0.123*** (0.037)	-0.104** (0.039)	-0.108*** (0.037)
Time Dependence Parameter	1.051 (0.100)	1.085 (0.110)	1.081 (0.110)	1.095 (0.130)	1.085 (0.120)	1.101 (0.110)	1.087 (0.120)	1.135 (0.140)	1.166 (0.120)
Log Likelihood[a]	-69.08 (54.0)	-66.51 (49.5)	-65.81 (70.4)	-69.76 (34.9)	-69.81 (35.0)	-64.36 (123.0)	-65.5 (105.4)	-63.98 (122.2)	-63.41 (119.0)
Observations	1140	1140	1140	1140	1140	1140	1140	1140	1140

Note: Robust standard errors, clustered on democratic episode, in parentheses.

*** $p < 0.01$, ** $p < 0.05$, * $p < 0.1$.

[a] Chi-squared statistic from a Wald test against a constant-only model in parentheses.

log GDP per capita and a dummy indicating the decade of democratization, as well as for government policy, as represented by government spending on consumption as a percentage of GDP.[9] In Table 2.8, we report our findings on how initial conditions and democratic reversal are related, controlling for economic performance (average GDP growth during the previous five years and log consumer price inflation), political institutions (constraints on executive power), and government policy. The sample used for the regressions reported in Table 2.8 was smaller than that used in Table 2.7 due to the more limited availability of data on, for example, income inequality. Table 2.9, making use of a further reduced sample because of the availability of data on foreign aid, contains the result of regressions assessing the relationship between government policy and democratic reversal, controlling for economic performance, political institutions, and initial conditions. Note that all our specifications significantly (at a 99 percent level) improve on a constant-only model, as indicated by a Wald test of the joint null hypothesis that all the coefficients in our model are equal to zero.

Beginning with the economic variables analyzed in Table 2.7, we see that higher GDP growth is significantly associated with a reduced probability of democratic reversal. Because the five-year average growth rate was associated with a notably larger reduction in risk of reversal, and was more consistently significant across specifications than individual year-on-year growth, we chose to include the average measure in the rest of our regressions. We also found that high rates of inflation *in any one year* were significantly associated with a substantial rise in the probability of democratic reversal in all specifications.[10]

---

[9] Data on GDP, inflation, investment, per-capita GDP, and government spending are from the WDI (2006). Executive constraints measured using the Polity IV score for constraints on executive power. Data on presidential versus parliamentary regimes was compiled from Przeworski et al. (2000) and the World Bank Database of Political Institutions.

[10] Because consumer price inflation ranged from −10 percent (in Sudan in 1968) to over 11,000 percent (Bolivia in 1986), we used the log of one plus the rate of inflation as our measure of inflation.

Our analysis of political institutions earlier in this chapter suggested that constraints on executive power, independent of the distinction between presidential and parliamentary democracies, had a marked relationship with democratic reversal. Our regression results provide further evidence of this relationship (note that endogeneity should not be a problem with this result as we are taking a component of the Polity IV score and regressing it against the probability of a *change* in that score). Although the Polity score for constraints on executive power was significant at the 10 percent level across most of our specifications, a dummy variable taking a value of 1 for presidential regimes was never significant. *We consequently reiterate that institutions providing checks and balances do appear to play a crucial role in whether young democracies consolidate or collapse.* However, our research also suggests that the most effective way to build such checks remains unclear and certainly merits a great deal more work. We discuss several aspects of this issue in the remaining chapters.

The variable "prior democratizations" in Table 2.7 takes a value of one if the episode of the democracy was the first in the country's history, two if it was the second attempt at democratic governance, and so on. At first glance, this measure of the country's previous experience with democracy does not appear to significantly affect the risk of democratic reversal. As an alternate and more sensitive measure of a country's prior experience with democratization, we also used a variable measuring the cumulative years of democracy that the country had experienced up to and including the present year.[11] This variable also showed no significant relationship with the risk of reversal. Thus, it seems that once we control for other factors influencing the success or failure of young democracies,

---

[11] More specifically, the variable "cumulative years of democracy" measured the total years of democracy, according to our measure, that a country had experienced from 1800 or its independence up to and including the year in question. This variable therefore resembles the measure of "domestic democratic capital" employed by Persson and Tabellini (2006), although we do not allow for depreciation as those authors do.

the apparent learning effects that some scholars have flagged may not in fact be particularly important for *young* democracies (Gerring et al. 2005, Persson and Tabellini 2006). Still, we remain somewhat agnostic on the question of whether "age matters" to the chances for democratic survival. This is because, in Tables 2.8 and 2.9, we see that the time-dependence parameter does in fact show as significant in some specifications. Our mixed results indicate that although there may be some institutional improvement or learning that occurs over time *within* a given democratization episode, we are not convinced that this is carried over from previous democratic experiments.

Turning our attention to Table 2.8, on the relationship between initial conditions and the risk of democratic reversal, we see that a higher initial level of GDP per capita is associated with a lower probability of reversal. This relationship is not only statistically significant at the one percent level for nearly all specifications but of a sizeable magnitude. However, when infant mortality is included, the coefficient on GDP per capita is no longer significant.[12] These two variables are in fact highly correlated (the correlation coefficient is above 0.75), and both presumably provide a broad indication of a country's level of development. Infant mortality in theory provides a better indication of how broadly the benefits of that development have been shared. We note, however, that the quality and frequency of data on GDP per capita were greater. For this reason, and because the magnitude of the coefficient on GDP per capita was significantly higher than that of infant mortality, we chose to include that indicator as a control for the level of development in the rest of our specifications. *Nonetheless, we do find that higher rates of infant mortality are significantly associated with a statistically significant increase in the risk of democratic reversal.*

As we would expect based on our discussions elsewhere in this volume, income inequality and ethnic fragmentation were both associated with increased risk of democratic reversal, but these relationships were

---

[12] Data on infant mortality per 1,000 live births is from the WDI (2006).

TABLE 2.8. *Initial conditions and risk of democratic reversal*

Regressions: Impact on Risk of Democratic Failure, Weibull Hazard Model
Reporting estimated % change in baseline hazard rate resulting from a one-unit increase in the independent variable

	(10)	(11)	(12)	(13)	(14)	(15)	(16)
Growth, 5-yr Ave.	−0.174***	−0.133***	−0.136***	−0.134***	−0.131***	−0.130***	−0.229***
	(0.041)	(0.044)	(0.045)	(0.047)	(0.046)	(0.045)	(0.058)
Log Inflation	0.220	0.272	0.323	0.266	0.282	0.286	0.528*
	(0.240)	(0.320)	(0.320)	(0.330)	(0.340)	(0.330)	(0.340)
Executive	−0.269**	−0.225*	−0.236*	−0.215	−0.218	−0.227*	−0.290**
Constraints	(0.097)	(0.120)	(0.120)	(0.120)	(0.120)	(0.120)	(0.110)
Log GDP per	−0.296	−0.628***	−0.593***	−0.634**	−0.639***	−0.637***	−0.550***
capita	(0.160)	(0.086)	(0.110)	(0.080)	(0.082)	(0.079)	(0.120)
Pre-1980	4.693***	8.024***	7.147***	8.031***	8.026***	7.896***	7.491***
	(2.690)	(3.970)	(3.690)	(4.290)	(4.410)	(3.730)	(3.730)
Infant Mortality	0.024***						
	(0.008)						
Gini Coefficient		0.031					
		(0.039)					
Ethnic				1.316			
				(3.110)			
Oil Dependent					−0.230		
					(0.740)		
Post-Colonial					−0.097		
					(0.470)		
World Growth						−0.018	
						(0.130)	
Lat. Am.							−0.727
							(0.230)
E. Europe							−0.970**
							(0.043)
Sub-Saharan							−0.301
Africa							(0.340)
Government	−0.133***	−0.139***	−0.144***	−0.141***	−0.138***	−0.141***	−0.164***
Consumption	(0.037)	(0.042)	(0.042)	(0.041)	(0.044)	(0.041)	(0.044)
(% GDP)							
Time Dependence	1.373***	1.179	1.176	1.185	1.189	1.177	1.273**
Parameter	(0.17)	(0.12)	(0.12)	(0.13)	(0.14)	(0.12)	(0.15)
Log Likelihood[a]	−51.37	−54.99	−54.94	−55.18	−55.22	−55.23	−52.43
	(91.1)	(98.8)	(84.4)	(113.9)	(101.4)	(101.7)	(94.8)
Observations	1052	1052	1052	1052	1052	1052	1052

Note: Robust standard errors, clustered on democratic episode, in parentheses.
*** $p < 0.01$, ** $p < 0.05$, * $p < 0.1$.
[a] Chi-squared statistic from a Wald test against a constant-only model in parentheses.

not statistically significant in our full sample (the next chapter discusses the roles these factors have played in particular regions, which have in fact been significant).[13] Dependence on oil is not significantly related with the overthrow of young democracies, and the sign associated with oil dependence is the opposite of what we would expect.[14] The conclusion that we draw from these findings is that regression results must be read in the context of looking at averages and relative weights across a broad cross section of countries, and that in particular cases these variables may be of great importance, as our descriptive statistics suggest. This is why, in the following chapter, we look more closely at regional case studies.

We find that regional effects for Africa and Latin America were not statistically significant (democracies here are not more likely to reverse, all other things being equal), and we did not include a regional dummy for Asia because of the heterogeneity of the region's democratizers, which we discuss in detail in Chapter 3. However, we do find that, ceteris paribus, democratizers in Eastern Europe faced a significantly lower risk of reversal than those found elsewhere, perhaps because of the "lock-in" effects of accession to the European Union.

The association between the *timing* of democratization and its success or failure is both statistically significant and of large magnitude, yet presents an important question as opposed to offering any answers. Democratizations that took place before 1980 appear to have faced a substantially larger chance of reversal than those in subsequent decades. Dummies for the 1980s, 1990s, and 2000s were tested but were not significantly associated with any change in the risk of democratic reversal. Dummy variables for the 1960s and 1970s, by contrast, were both significant, and because a Wald test failed to reject the null that their

---

[13] Inequality data come from the University of Texas Inequality Project. Ethnic fragmentation data are from Alesina et al. (2003).

[14] Countries where oil rents account for more than 10 percent of GDP were flagged as oil dependent, based on data from the WDI (2006).

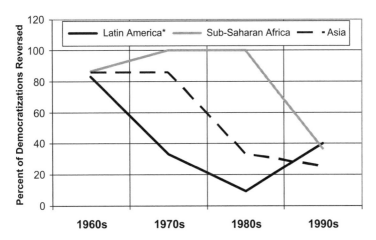

FIGURE 2.10. Reversal Rates Over Time. *Upturn in 1990s due to two failed democratizations in Haiti. *Source:* Polity IV, authors' calculations.

coefficients were identical, we include a single variable, flagging democratizations that occurred before to 1980.

As Table 2.8 makes clear, this relationship remains significant even when we include regional dummies in our model, indicating that the higher probability of success in the post-1980 period is not due to the fact that, for example, Eastern European states that emerged from communist rule had a greater chance of maintaining democratic rule. Indeed, we can see in Figure 2.10 that the rate at which democracies fail declined in *all* regions in the post-1980 period. A young democracy was more likely to survive during the 1990s than during the 1970s, regardless of the region.

We also considered several other factors that changed over the period in question. Suspecting that the significance of the timing variable was driven by difficulties experienced by postcolonial democratizers, we included a dummy flagging democratizations immediately following independence from colonial rule, but as Table 2.8 shows, the timing variable remained highly significant. One might expect the global economic environment to have some affect on the probability of democratic survival, but the timing variable was still significant and of a large magnitude when we controlled for the rate of world output growth (see Table 2.8). In the previous section, we noted that descriptive statistics raised the possibility that the timing effect was due to an increase in foreign aid, but in Table 2.9, we see that the pre-1980 dummy variable remains highly significant even when we control for levels of foreign aid. Factors such as the advance of globalization or a change in U.S. foreign policy may help explain this change in the success of democracies over time. In Chapter 5, we examine some of these factors and suggest how further research might illuminate this issue.

As we discussed in the previous section, the question of whether young democracies can or should implement economic reforms has been hotly debated. To assess whether shifts in economic policy were associated with democratic reversal, we included as a regressor trade, as a percentage of GDP, as well as a dummy variable taking a value of one after the democratic government liberalized the economy (as indicated by the Sachs–Warner openness measure).[15] We also include as a regressor government consumption spending, as a percentage of GDP, and the amount foreign aid the country received, as a percentage of GDP.[16]

Table 2.9 summarizes our findings regarding the effects of policy on the survival of young democracies. Spending seems to matter, as higher government consumption was associated with a significantly lower risk of reversal.[17] At the same time, not only do more open economies appear to face a lower risk of reversal, but we also found a significant *negative* relationship between liberalization and the rate at which democratic governments were overthrown.[18] *Thus, we do not find support for the*

---

[15] Data on trade as a percentage of GDP is from the WDI (2006), whereas data on Sachs–Warner openness is from Wacziarg and Horn Welch (2003).

[16] Aid data are from the WDI (2006).

[17] This result did not change when we used various measures of the *change* in government consumption during the period of democracy.

[18] We also tested the model with the change in trade as a percentage of GDP. This did not affect the basic results.

TABLE 2.9. *Government policies and risk of democratic reversal*

Regressions: Impact on Risk of Democratic Failure, Weibull Hazard Model
Reporting estimated % change in baseline hazard rate resulting from a
one-unit increase in the independent variable

	(16)	(17)	(18)	(19)
Growth, 5yr Ave	−0.053*	−0.072**	−0.051	−0.05*
	(0.029)	(0.031)	(0.030)	(0.029)
Log Inflation	0.895***	0.85***	0.773***	0.940***
	(0.330)	(0.340)	(0.330)	(0.340)
Executive Constraints	−0.174*	−0.172*	−0.154*	−0.180*
	(0.097)	(0.092)	(0.100)	(0.094)
Log GDP per capita	−0.559***	−0.548***	−0.555***	−0.604***
	(0.085)	(0.083)	(0.088)	(0.093)
Pre-1980	6.213***	6.141***	4.395***	5.524***
	(2.430)	(2.420)	(1.880)	(2.250)
Government	−0.086***	−0.064**	−0.094***	−0.078**
Consumption	(0.030)	(0.030)	(0.029)	(0.031)
Trade (%GDP)		−0.016*		
		(0.009)		
Liberalization			−0.735***	
			0.130	
Aid (%GDP)				−(0.021)
				(0.023)
Time Dependence	1.073	1.214	1.260**	1.108
Parameter	(0.110)	(0.150)	(0.140)	(0.120)
Log Likelihood[a]	−72.1	−69.56	−68.21	−71.53
	(106.0)	(72.4)	(111.4)	(103.3)
Observations	987	987	987	987

Note: Robust standard errors, clustered on democratic episode, in parentheses.
*** p < 0.01, ** p < 0.05, * p < 0.1.
[a] Chi-squared statistic from a Wald test against a constant-only model in parentheses.

proposition that economic reforms such as the liberalization of trade provoke a backlash that can undermine young democracies.

Finally, we look at the policies of donor governments and find that more foreign aid is associated with a lower probability of reversal. Naturally, here there could be problems of endogeneity at work: more aid is given in the first place to countries that are less likely to fail. We do not probe that issue in any detail here, particularly as the relationship in our model is not statistically significant. Moreover, as already noted, the direction of causality is also open to question.

Conclusions

To summarize our empirical findings, we find some evidence in our descriptive statistics that initial conditions do significantly affect the chances that democracy will be sustained, although evidence from the regression analysis is more mixed. Newly democratic regimes in countries with low per-capita income and high infant mortality rates appear to face a higher risk of being overthrown, a finding that would seem to support modernization theory (for a recent defense, see Epstein et al. 2006). However, we emphasize that many countries have managed to overcome these barriers to create apparently durable democratic institutions if not on their first then on subsequent democratization attempts.

We also find that a number of institutional variables play a crucial role in determining whether democracy is sustained. Following many other scholars cited earlier, for example, we would agree that the risk of reversal is reduced the longer a democratic regime is in place, possibly suggesting that robust democratic institutions take time to develop. Our regression analysis further highlights that effective checks on executive power substantially increase the chances that democracy will survive, although a parliamentary system of government does not appear to guarantee that such checks exist, contrary to much of the received wisdom.

Finally, we wish to stress that although characteristics such as ethnic fragmentation and income inequality do not appear as statistically significant in our regressions, this does not imply that policy-makers (or scholars for that matter) should dismiss these factors as wholly unimportant. Beyond the obvious data limitations with respect to these variables, we also wish to stress that the other factors we have discussed here are more significant when we look at all our data *on average*. In any *particular* country case, in contrast, ethnic divisions or income inequality may play a very crucial role in determining the fate of a young democratic government.[19] For this reason, in the following chapter we focus on the precise factors that seem to be at work either supporting or undermining democracy in the world's developing regions.

---

[19] We thank Jack Goldstone of George Mason University for highlighting this important shortcoming of regression analysis.

3 Are Some Regions More Democracy Friendly?

> Democracy is the most realistic way for diverse peoples to resolve their differences, and share power, and heal social divisions....
>
> U.S. Secretary of State Condoleezza Rice (keynote address at the World Economic Forum, January 23, 2008)

ONE OF THE MOST SIGNIFICANT FINDINGS TO EMERGE FROM our descriptive statistics concerns the considerable cross-country and cross-regional variation we observe with respect to the economic performance and political durability of young democracies. Thus, democracy in Eastern Europe and Latin America has generally moved (with some important exceptions we discuss later) toward consolidation, whereas in East Asia and Africa it has faced greater difficulty taking root. Why is that the case? What explains this diversity in the prospects for democratic survival?

In this chapter we explore these questions from a regional perspective. Naturally, we do not pretend to offer a detailed history of the political economy of each part of the developing world; instead, following a pioneering article by Krieckhaus (2006), we highlight the effects of the "initial conditions" commonly associated with particular places – for example, income and asset inequality in Latin America and ethnolinguistic fragmentation in Africa – on subsequent political and economic developments following the shift to a democratic polity. Although some of the variables we focus on in what follows do not necessarily loom large in our regression analysis, they do emerge as significant in the context of particular countries and this reminds us of the importance of conducting in-depth case study research alongside large-N data analysis.

If "initial conditions", as broadly defined, influence the prospects for democratic consolidation, the specific pressures they place on leaders need to be clearly understood. At the same time, it should be recognized that self-interested politicians might exploit these conditions – like ethnic fragmentation – to advance their own careers, even at the expense of building nascent democratic institutions. Because of this "two-way street," we are not convinced that initial conditions determine outcomes on their own; after all, if they did, how would we explain the eventual success of the many repeat democratizers in our data set? Apparently, the choices that political leaders make – along with the type and quality of support provided by the international community – matter as well. One can only imagine, for example, how different South Africa's trajectory might have been without the leadership of a Nelson Mandela or how Central and Eastern Europe would have fared without the transition support of the European Union.

Further, we have observed in earlier chapters that the *age* of democracy – can have a positive influence on future prospects. To put this as an empirical proposition, the older the democracy, the higher the likelihood a state will remain democratic in the future. Thus, one variation we might observe across regions with respect to democratic consolidation or its absence is simply because of the amount of time that countries have enjoyed democracy. And in addition to this historical experience, we have observed in earlier chapters that, as a general rule, democracies that emerged after 1980 had a better chance of surviving than those that appeared during the 1960s or 1970s; more on this in our concluding chapter where we discuss topics for future research.

What these comments suggest is that the rules determining how democratic institutions operate, the sorts of policy decisions (for example, with respect to income and asset redistribution) that leaders actually make, and the degree of international support that a young democracy receives, all interact with initial conditions to shape a regime's chances for survival. Thus, we agree with Fish when he writes, "polities undergoing regime change do not necessarily suffer under a tyranny of initial conditions. They make their own fates" (Fish 2001, 82). But if political choices do matter to democratic consolidation, then the policy community will need to pay closer attention to the variables, both institutional and economic, that can be manipulated in the hope of helping young democratizers consolidate. With this in mind, we now turn to our discussion of regional experiences, beginning with a brief recapitulation of our economic evidence to set the stage for the analysis that follows.

The Economics of Young Democracies: A Regional Perspective

As already noted, young democracies have varied greatly in their ability to deliver stable long-run growth, and a wealth of evidence suggests that poor performance provides one (if not the only) signal that democratic backsliding and reversal may not be far away (again, one of our contributions in this book is to examine some of the institutional variables that might cause, among other pathologies, poor economic performance to begin with). Changes in key economic indicators in new democracies follow quite different trajectories in different regions, a finding in line with those of Krieckhaus (2006), who contends that democracy's economic impact varies by region.

To recapitulate our findings, and beginning with the broadest measure of economic growth, the performance of Eastern European countries differs significantly from that of other new democracies, with output contracting sharply in the first two to three years after democratization and growth resuming thereafter, presumably caused by the specific circumstances of the transition from Communism. Democratization in both Latin America and sub-Saharan Africa, in contrast, appears to bring about a significant "democracy dividend" when it comes to

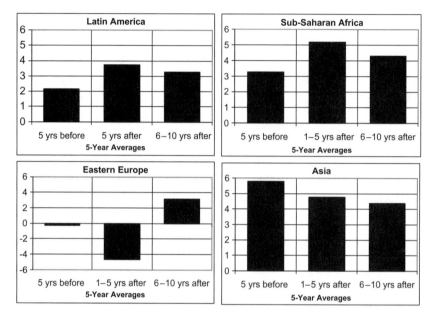

FIGURE 3.1. Regional Variation in GDP Growth Before and After Democratization. *Source:* WDI, Polity IV, authors' calculations. *Note:* Five years before and after denotes the average for the period 1–5 years; 5–10 denotes the average for the five years from year 6 through year 10.

economic growth. *These sharply different growth trajectories across regions, evident in Figure 3.1, coupled with the differences in democratic survival across regions (which we discuss in detail later), demonstrate the difficulty in drawing broad generalizations about the economic performance of young democracies and their chances of consolidation or reversal.*

Interestingly, average growth for new democracies in sub-Saharan Africa outperforms the average for all young democracies, as well as the regional average for Latin America. This result is in part a product of the strong performance of newly independent democracies in the region during the 1960s, a period of robust growth worldwide. If cases classified as new democracies at independence are excluded from the African

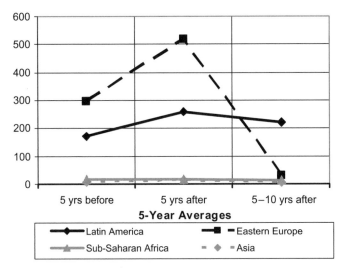

FIGURE 3.2. Average Inflation in Young Democracies. *Source:* WDI, Polity IV, authors' calculations.

group, average growth falls by a percentage point or more, although the trajectory remains the same. Moreover, when we consider the difference between the growth rate of young democracies during their first five years and the growth of global output during the same period, we find that new African democracies grew slightly faster than the world total, whereas Latin American countries lagged behind world growth. This suggests that the regional differences in the growth performance of young democracies are not simply a product of the timing of democratization.

Moving to macroeconomic policy, we have found that Latin America's new democracies have been plagued by high and volatile inflation, even 10 years after democratization (though recent years have seen more success with stabilization). By contrast, Eastern European states faced high and variable inflation immediately after the transition to democracy, but in that region inflation levels have since moderated to reasonably low and stable levels (see Figure 3.2). Average inflation in Africa, in contrast, has rarely exceeded 10 percent, a finding that might surprise some casual observers of the continent's economic policies, who associate that region with policy instability and chronically bad performance borne of volatile commodity prices and generally poor governance structures.

To summarize, the economic performance of the world's youngest democracies has not converged but seems to vary significantly across regions. In the following sections we try to understand why that is the case and what its consequences have been for democratic consolidation. We begin our analysis with Latin America before turning to Eastern Europe, Africa, and Asia.

Latin America: The Political Economy of Populism

As just noted, Latin America's young democracies have experienced high and variable rates of inflation, whereas their growth performance has lagged that of other regions. Moreover, numerous financial crises have hit countries throughout Latin America since the late 1970s, further highlighting the region's economic instability. Economic performance has varied widely, both over time within nations and across countries. Even if one looks only at new democracies in the region, variance in economic performance is striking. Whereas the return to democracy in Chile brought stability and economic prosperity, nascent democratic governments in Brazil, Argentina, and Peru have been plagued by a host of economic problems (see Figure 3.3).

Although governments in the region appear to have finally tamed inflation – in 2006, no country in the region had inflation over 15 percent – growth continues to disappoint. A recent report from the UN Economic Commission on Latin America and the Caribbean noted, "although the region's growth rates are high from a historical standpoint, they fall short of the rates being marked up in other parts of the developing world" (Economic Commission on Latin America and the Caribbean 2006). Moreover, Latin America's high levels of poverty and income inequality mean that the benefits of the region's recent moderate

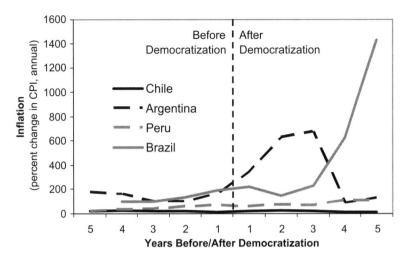

FIGURE 3.3. Inflation Before and After Democratization.

success have not yet translated into widespread improvements in living standards.

Despite this disappointing economic performance, Latin America's democracies have proved remarkably durable, again posing a puzzle for those who draw strong causal connections between the two. Of the 25 cases of democratization we count on the continent, only nine have been reversed, giving the region a far higher percentage of survivors than either Africa or Asia (see Table 3.1). Nevertheless, we continue to be concerned about the fate of democracy in Latin America for two reasons in particular. First, public demands for widespread improvement in living standards have historically led Latin American governments to pursue policies that, while perhaps delivering benefits in the short run, come at the expense of long-run growth and stability, both political and economic. Second, efforts by politicians, irrespective of ideology, to sweep aside institutional constraints in search of "quick fixes" to their countries' economic problems have often found substantial popular support. Thus, although democracy has endured in Latin America, in this section we argue that it remains malleable, prone to backsliding if not

TABLE 3.1. *Democratizations in Latin America*

Country	Year of democratization	Year of reversal (if any)
Dominican Republic	1962	1963
Trinidad	1962	
Dominican Republic	1978	
Haiti	1990	1991
Haiti	1994	1999
Guatemala	1966	1970
Honduras	1982	
El Salvador	1984	
Guatemala	1986	
Panama	1989	
Nicaragua	1990	
Mexico	1997	
Peru	1963	1968
Guyana	1966	1978
Ecuador	1968	1970
Argentina	1973	1976
Ecuador	1979	
Peru	1980	1992
Bolivia	1982	
Argentina	1983	
Brazil	1985	
Uruguay	1985	
Paraguay	1989	
Chile	1989	
Guyana	1992	
Peru	2001	

outright reversal, as such contemporary cases as Bolivia and Venezuela
(the latter being an "old" as opposed to a "young" democracy) make
clear.

In seeking to understand the Latin American experience, Krieckhaus has observed that a "central theme in the... literature" is that the
region's high levels of income inequality (an "initial condition") have
generated a distinctive set of pressures on political leaders, who are ever
fearful of social instability and even political revolution. As he explains,
"The standard argument is that severe economic inequality... motivates

politicians to promise higher wages and increased government spending, which in turn generates economic crises" (Krieckhaus 2006, 320). While we agree that preexisting levels of inequality have contributed to Latin America's economic volatility, we argue that shortcomings in the region's political institutions have also played a crucial, independent role in generating the boom/bust cycles in its economic performance. Specifically, following a line of research developed by Fish (2001) and Weyland (2002, 2003), we argue that both economic reform and democratic governance tend to be weakest in those countries that adopt what Fish terms *super-presidential* systems of power. If this finding seemingly supports the view that parliamentary regimes do a better job of checking executive power, especially in developing countries, it is important to bear in mind the evidence we have presented in earlier chapters that parliamentary systems provide no guarantees against democratic reversal. Instead, it is the *effectiveness* of checks and balances rather than the specific constitutional structure that is of central importance to democratic consolidation and sustained economic growth, and we certainly recognize that the degree of effectiveness arises not just from formal institutions – after all, many countries around the world share constitutional arrangements that look good on paper – but also, as noted earlier, from the informal institutions of civil society, including, *inter alia*, a free press, vibrant nongovernmental organizations, private sector firms, professional associations, labor unions, educational systems, and so forth. Still, our emphasis here is on formal institutional arrangements.

Economic inequality, when combined with "strong" presidential systems, has forged in Latin America a unique brand of "macroeconomic populism." Karen Remmer (1993), for example, has noted that Latin American economies exhibit pronounced political business cycles (PBCs), and these cycles peak not *before* elections, as predicted by the relevant PBC literature, but in the first year or two *after* a new government has taken office. Rather than invest in such public goods as health and education to ameliorate poverty and inequality over the long run, newly elected governments have instead used expansionary fiscal and monetary policies to boost real wages and the share of labor in national income, with impressive success over periods of one to three years but at the price of sustained and stable growth (Sachs 1989; Dornbusch and Edwards 1991). Indeed, after three years or so, such policies invariably bring about an economic correction that carries disastrous consequences for the intended beneficiaries.

This policy trajectory has been followed not only by presidents identified as "populist" in the broader sense of the term, including Juan Peron in Argentina and Alan Garcia (during his first term in office) in Peru, but also by many others, such as Jose Sarney in Brazil. Indeed, one could also view Carlos Menem's implementation of a currency board system in Argentina as an example of this tendency to adopt "quick fixes" to economic problems at the expense of long-term viability.

The "quick fix" phenomenon can be understood as a response to what Phillip Keefer has called *political market failures* in young democratizers (Keefer 2007a). When political credibility is scarce – that is, when voters doubt the ability of politicians to deliver on their promises, like income or land redistribution, as is quite likely in newly democratic states – elected leaders do not have the luxury of adopting policies that will benefit their constituents only several years into the future if they wish to remain in office. Voters will simply not believe their assertions that the benefits from a given set of policies are forthcoming, and they may vote leaders out of office or take to the streets in the meantime. Thus, in Bolivia and repeatedly in Ecuador, presidents have been forced out of office in midterm by protesters who have found their policies wanting.

Institutions such as well-functioning political parties clearly have a role to play in mitigating the economic volatility that has plagued Latin America, by providing politicians with needed credibility. They do so by providing direct links between political leaders and voters, giving the former the leeway necessary to pursue policies that will bear fruit only in the medium or long run (World Bank 2005). However, political dynamics in the region have impeded the development of such institutions and eroded existing ones, for reasons we will now discuss.

Frustration at the lack of widespread improvement in living standards in Latin America has not only led to the adoption of ultimately counter-productive "quick fix" economic policies but, even more perniciously, has served to generate substantial popular support for efforts by presidents of all stripes to sweep aside institutional constraints on executive power, purportedly to give them the policy space to tackle pressing problems. We believe that such efforts put democracy at risk in the region, as well as impede improvement in economic policymaking.

In response to economic crisis, widespread poverty, or other social problems, presidents ranging from Alberto Fujimori in Peru and Carlos Menem in Argentina to Hugo Chavez in Venezuela and Evo Morales in Bolivia (and many more) have sought to reduce or eliminate formal institutional constraints on presidential authority to pursue their respective agendas unfettered. In Fujimori's case, the president dissolved Congress to press ahead with rapid privatization and other economic reforms and to prosecute a war against Maoist insurgents. More recently, Venezuelan President Hugo Chavez has secured authorization from his nation's congress to rule by decree for an 18-month period, citing the need to accelerate the pace of socialist-oriented policy reform. As Rabello de Castro and Ronci emphasize in their analysis of Brazil, "Populism hates limits to the ruler's power that sound institutions would otherwise bring about" (1991, 168), although we note that this desire to do away with checks and balances has not been limited to avowedly populist leaders in the region.

Kurt Weyland has noted that efforts to erode controls on executive power have also extended beyond formal institutions. Thus, powerful presidents have sought to weaken their opponents' organizational bases to enhance their own latitude for action. Such attempts to "weaken and divide 'veto players'" have included rhetorical and legal attacks on business federations, labor unions, and other politically active organizations

(Weyland 2002, 142). The resulting weakening of *de facto* constraints has had a further a negative effect on democratic development.

Apart from its impact on democracy, the preference of Latin American presidents for greater autonomy at the expense of institutions has also had negative consequences for economic management in the region. Although positive reforms were carried out across the region during the 1980s and 1990s, the "bitter pill" of economic stabilization and structural adjustment (Weyland 1998) was rarely followed by the so-called second-generation reforms necessary to accelerate growth and bring about widespread improvement in living standards. In the absence of measures institutionalizing or "locking in" economic reforms, fears that a change of administration may bring about a radical change in economic orientation persist. For example, in the run-up to the election of Luiz Ignacio Lula da Silva in Brazil in 2002, spreads on the country's bonds spiked, with negative repercussions for the country's economy (for more on this issue, see Block 2005). Failure to institutionalize policy produces endogenous economic instability. Even if politicians do not manipulate macro variables, the expectation that government policies will change can introduce volatility into economic performance.[1]

We thus find that a negative feedback loop appears to be at work in Latin America. Frustration with a lack of economic progress breeds popular support for the erosion of institutional checks on executive authority. The resulting undermining of political parties and other organizations fosters political market failures that force newly elected leaders to pursue policies that sacrifice medium-term growth in favor of short-term benefits for their supporters. Economic troubles, in turn, lead to greater frustration with government.

Recent events provide a clear illustration of this dynamic. Political scientists agree that one of the factors preventing effective policy-making in Ecuador is the absence of well-functioning political parties. Nonetheless, in 2002 and again in 2006, voters elected to the presidency

---

[1] We thank Karen Remmer for emphasizing this point.

candidates blaming the country's woes on its few, small political parties, and promising to further reduce the power of these parties. This process has produced a fragmented legislature that cannot act as an effective counterweight to the presidency and that cannot enact needed reforms.

At once troubling and challenging to those who seek to promote economic stability and democracy in the region is the fact that these efforts have routinely met with widespread public support. A newly elected populist leader like Bolivian President Morales, for example, can draw confidence from the examples of Fujimori, Menem, and Chavez, who were all reelected by wide margins after doing away with constraints on executive power. Although the case of Ecuador – where both Abdala Bucaram's attempts to concentrate power in his own hands and Lucio Gutierrez's sacking of the entire Supreme Court provoked massive demonstrations that ultimately led to the ouster of these presidents – suggests that under certain circumstances citizens will act to defend independent institutions, the overall outlook in the region is not encouraging. Unless voters themselves value assertive legislatures and independent judiciaries, it is not entirely clear what can be done, for example, by the international community to ensure the building and maintenance of institutional checks and balances.

In fact, the interaction of political institutions and economic policy that we have highlighted presents the international community with a dilemma. On the one hand, presidents in the region might be supported for undertaking economic reforms that are widely perceived as necessary and beneficial; on the other, they might do so in a way that undermines political institutions. Do the ends thus justify the means? We would assert that they do not. Checks and balances on policy-makers are crucial for both economic development and democratic survival. Damage to political and governmental institutions may take a long time to undo, and that damage can do severe harm to a country's long-run prospects.

This argument resonates with recent empirical work that emphasizes the role of good institutions in fostering development (Acemoglu, Johnson, and Robinson 2005). From that perspective, it is entirely possible that the negative impact of undermining constitutional structures over the long run outweighs the immediate gains from any economic reforms made possible by circumventing the legislature or judiciary. Further, as these institutions are undermined and the system of checks and balances jettisoned, the likelihood of democratic reversal increases. It is for these reasons that we view the ongoing political developments in at least several Latin American states with concern.

Eastern Europe: Democratizing During Hard Times

If democratic reversals were caused mainly by economic collapse, as much of the political economy literature has claimed, surely no region's democracies would have faced greater threats in modern times than those of post-communist Eastern Europe. The fall of the Berlin Wall in 1989 symbolized not only the end of Soviet domination in that part of the world but also the onset of an economic collapse that is rivaled in its scale only by the Great Depression of the 1930s. Industrial production plummeted across Central and Eastern Europe by between 15 percent and 40 percent, whereas unemployment – which was virtually unknown under Communism – jumped to 30 percent or more of the active population. States that had once provided their citizens with "cradle-to-grave" social services, if only poorly, now reneged on their obligations to society's most vulnerable persons. As a consequence, poverty skyrocketed while at the same time a few privileged insiders were getting rich from the economic transition and the opportunities it presented, both for entrepreneurship and for the capture of illicit rents. Institutions at every level failed to provide oversight or a modicum of regulation, and countless individuals lost their life savings in the Ponzi schemes that spread across the region. All the ingredients, it would seem, were therefore present for widespread democratic reversals.

But the difficulties of making meaningful generalizations about the relationship between economic policy and performance on the one hand and democratic consolidation on the other are perhaps most strikingly

TABLE 3.2. *Democratizations in Eastern Europe*[a]

Country	Year of democratization	Year of reversal (if any)
Hungary	1990	
Czech Republic	1990	
Bulgaria	1990	
Romania	1990	
Poland	1991	
Albania	1992	
Macedonia	1991	
Slovenia	1991	
Moldova	1991	
Croatia	2000	
Yugoslavia	2000	
Estonia	1991	
Latvia	1991	
Lithuania	1991	
Ukraine	1991	
Belarus	1991	1995
Armenia	1991	1995
Georgia	1991	
Russia	1992	
Slovakia	1993	
Armenia	1998	

[a] We remind readers that we include only those nations that, according to the Polity IV data, underwent a democratization. Thus, we do not include here those states – mainly in Central Asia – that were never considered democratic following the collapse of the Soviet Union. Further, we do not list here the "backsliders" that are still nominally democratic. That list would include, notably, Russia.

apparent in the case of the post-communist nations of Eastern Europe. We witness in this region such a wide range of economic and political outcomes as to make any sweeping statements suspect. Since 1989, several former communist countries have reformed their economies and polities to such an extent as to have become members of the European Union. Others, like Armenia, Belarus, and Russia (not counted as a democratic reversal in our data set, which ends in 2004), must unfortunately be considered reversed democracies where a return to something like authoritarian rule is either threatened or has for all practical purposes already occurred (see Table 3.2).

What explains this variation over democratic outcomes across the post-Soviet world? Although we believe that initial conditions, such as the presence of oil resources and ethnic diversity, play a large role in explaining whether democracy has taken root (more on this later), we also note the crucial importance of the institutional choices that countries have made during the transition years. Armenia, for example, is an ethnically homogenous country and one "free" of oil, yet it has struggled to consolidate its nascent democratic institutions. It is interesting to note that the U.S. Department of State believes this is due to the high concentration of power held by the president, which the legislature has been unable to reduce (Armenia, *Background Note*, available on www.state. gov). Again, this may have reflected a widespread belief, held both by the international community and by domestic officials, that "strong" presidents in the post-Soviet sphere could drive through desperately needed economic reforms quickly, but such institutional designs come at the price of longer run democratic consolidation.

It is thus interesting to note in the Armenian context that the United States Agency for International Development (USAID), among other donor agencies, has focused its governance programs in recent years on building effective political parties in that country – and more broadly across the post-Soviet space. These parties, USAID believes, can contribute both to improved economic and political performance (see www.armenia.usaid.gov). This policy approach seems to recognize that strong presidents may not, after all, be the best instrument for advancing political and economic reform. As Kopstein (2003) has argued, "highly structured party systems...facilitate the adoption of public policies that foster economic growth...The alternative is a weakly structured system of...parties that are the playthings of charismatic leaders...."

The issue at stake in the former Soviet Union, therefore, is not so much the timing of reform policies as their institutionalization (or lack thereof). We thus reject the well-known analysis put forward, say, by Bresser Pereira, Maravall and Przeworski (1993), that rapid reform destabilized the allegedly fragile democracies of post-communist Eastern Europe. To the contrary, we agree with Fish (2001) when he states that "economic reform is...closely and positively related to democratization" *in those cases* where it is firmly institutionalized in constitutional structures with effective checks and balances and in independent central banks, judiciaries, and other market-enhancing agencies, including those found in civil society. Fish suggests that economic liberalization is beneficial to young democracies to the extent that it helps promote

> *the pluralization of economic power in a regime in which economic power was until recently both fused with political power and highly concentrated.* Rapid liberalization helps to pluralize economic power, thereby creating a firmer financial basis for the emergence and development of nonstate organizations that can check the growth of executive absolutism. Conversely, the nonpluralization of economic power restricts the growth potential of societal organizations, including opposition parties. (Fish 2001, 82; italics added)

In fact, Fish finds that *organized, programmatic parties are absent not only in the region's autocratic regimes but also in its democratic "backsliders."*

The connection that Fish highlights between centralized economic and political power fits well with the findings that Beck and Laeven (2005) have recently presented in a study for the World Bank. They provide a rich array of empirical evidence in support of the hypothesis that the presence of abundant natural resources in the former communist states helps to explain the fate of both democracy and economic performance in each. Again, initial conditions undoubtedly matter for both economic and political development, even if good institutional and policy choices can mitigate their malign effects.[2]

---

[2] Beck and Laeven are actually interested in the building of institutions more broadly defined, but one of the indicators they use to measure "institutions" is the Polity measure of executive constraints (2005, 20).

Thus, oil-rich economies like Russia and the Central Asian republics have been among those where democracy has had the greatest difficulty taking root, though of course Belarus (like Armenia) provides another non-resource-rich example of democracy being stifled by a strong president. In Russia and Central Asia, however, where oil is plentiful, the concentration of economic resources has undoubtedly been a driving force behind the centralization of political power, limiting competition in both spheres and creating what is now commonly called the "natural resources curse." *Beck and Laeven (2005) also show that where constraints on the executive were initially weak following the transition from Communism, economic performance – not only over the short run but even 10 years later – was inferior.*[3] The finding that the concentration of economic power facilitates the centralization of political power, which in turn has a negative impact on economic performance, highlights the shadow that initial conditions can cast over polities, as powerful incentives are created for rent-grabbing as opposed to the making of long-term investments.

The presence of rent-grabbing political elites comes at a cost to both the economy and the democratic future. As noted in the previous section on Latin America, several analysts have noted that the transformation of the executive office into a "super-presidency" cripples the very institutions that provide economic reform with its enduring foundations or prevents such institutions from ever seeing the light of day (Fish 2001; Weyland 2002). This institutional structure, in turn, makes the emergence of stable democracies less likely.

Given the former Soviet Union's totalitarian legacy, it is perhaps not surprising that several former communist nations in particular have

---

[3] Although they do not look specifically at the issue of executive constraints, Dethier, Ghanem, and Zoli (1999) and Fidrmuc (2001) also find that higher levels of democracy are associated with more extensive economic reform and, in turn, superior economic performance. Both studies employ the Freedom House measure of democracy, which places a premium on limits on executive power, although it does not provide a specific measure of these.

maintained authoritarian regimes or moved back in that direction. But this is not due solely to the domestic politics of each country; international influences have also mattered in this case, even if such influences are not always conducive to democracy-building. With respect to Eastern Europe, for example, Weyland (1999) suggests that presidents may have been especially tempted to reject limits on their power when they could "free ride" on their country's political-economic relationship with Russia, as with Alexander Lukashenko in Belarus or Leonid Kuchma in Ukraine, where the governments of the day won, for example, subsidized energy prices from Moscow. Thus, international influences in these cases (i.e., the continuing influence of Russia) provoked an authoritarian rather than a democratic lock-in, reminding us that the international system is not always benign for the world's young democracies (a point that we will reconsider in the Chapter 5 when we think, for example, of the consequences of a continuing Chinese ascendance on the democratic future). At the same time, democracy has also failed to take root in some states that did not depend so heavily on Moscow's largesse, like oil-rich Kazakhstan, again providing an example of the "natural resources curse."

Instead of falling under Russia's spell, several other Eastern European states, even during the bleakest years of economic crisis, immediately grasped the promise of joining the European Union (EU) and sought to anchor their political and economic reforms within that regional body. That promise enabled their leaders and supporters to gain the upper hand in policy debates by holding out carrots to a diversity of interest groups, particularly where illiberal solutions to policy issues provided tempting alternatives. In Estonia, for example, the government's treatment of the Russian minority might have taken an ugly turn, including the passage of blatantly discriminatory legislation and regulation, had it not been for the EU (not to mention Russia) staring over the government's shoulder. Overall, the EU bolstered the forces working on behalf of democracy and tolerant societies (but see Larrabee 2006 on the limits of European influence).

In terms of the economy, EU lock-in meant that both foreign and domestic investors could expect democratic consolidation alongside relatively stable economic policies, and this combination provided them with confidence. The rough treatment of foreign investors in Russia as compared to, for instance, Hungary, is telling in this regard. In some fields, authority over economic policy would eventually be taken away from governments altogether, such as monetary policy in those states that would adopt the Euro as their currency or trade policy, which is a competence of the European Commission in Brussels and not the member-states. Thus, external institutions have helped to constrain executive power, and super-presidentialism has posed less of a threat to the dual processes of economic and political development in the EU accession states.

Overall, then, the post-communist states provide some unique puzzles when it comes to the relationship between economics and politics. Although scholars might have expected the post-Soviet economic crisis to stifle the process of democratization or even reverse it, this has occurred in only a few states, mainly – though not exclusively – those with heavy concentrations of oil or high degrees of ethnic fragmentation. Further, democratic reversal and backsliding has been supported in several instances by Russia, as Moscow has made a renewed bid to increase its regional power.

The intermingling of economic and political power in countries like Russia has clearly been deleterious for democracy. In the places where this has happened, economic reforms were strangled at a relatively early stage to the benefit of political insiders who have profited mightily from privatization and liberalization, and through the granting of special privileges from the state. Simultaneously, Russia, among other states – and again, not just oil-rich states – witnessed a rise in presidential authority that has checked the development and independence of other democratic institutions. Ironically, this rise in power was aided and abetted in some instances by western aid programs, including International Monetary Fund packages, which sought to "strengthen the state" and its "autonomy." Unfortunately, as we have also seen in the Latin American case, super-presidencies are generally associated with a lack of credibility when it comes to the making of stable economic policies, translating into uneven economic performance while undermining democratic consolidation.

In sum, almost all the post-communist states saw a growth collapse of Great Depression magnitudes in the early 1990s. Since then, however, growth has generally improved while inflation levels have come down and stabilized. For many countries, this has been accompanied by democratic consolidation and regular, contested elections, along with the growth of civil liberties, a free press, the flowering of nongovernmental organizations, and the other attributes associated with modern, liberal democracy. For others, in contrast, the early economic crises were seized on by leaders as an excuse to strengthen the presidency at the expense of other governmental bodies and civil society. In these cases, neither sustained economic growth nor democratization is assured, given the paucity of durable institutional structures.

This analysis suggests that would-be democratizers – and those in the international community seeking to support them – should focus on the pluralization of both economic and political power as they promote reform and transition processes. Without such pluralization, super-presidents and their cronies will threaten the democratic future as they grab the rents that come from their stranglehold on the economy. Political parties, independent central banks and judiciaries, and a vibrant free press and civil society are among the best guarantors of a prosperous democratic future – alongside an international community that is willing to lend young democracies its support.

Africa: On the Road to Sustainable Development?

It is probably fair to say that no region of the world has attracted such bad press over the years as sub-Saharan Africa. From an economic perspective, the region is commonly viewed as having experienced a "growth tragedy" during the modern era (Easterly and Levine 1997) and it continues to witness human suffering in all its many cruel dimensions, both natural and human-made. As a result, Africa has become the focal point of both public and private international development efforts in recent years, with a variety of remedies and elixirs for Africa's problems – such as the need to double foreign aid or erase the burden of international debt payments – being offered up not only by academics and public officials but also by celebrities and pundits as well. It seems that everyone feels that they have to offer a solution for Africa's travails.

In this section, we review explanations for Africa's difficulties that have particular relevance for young democracies and then outline a number of reasons (in contrast to many analysts) as to why the outlook for political and economic development is improving – undoubtedly a bold statement in light of, for example, the interethnic violence that followed the flawed presidential election in Kenya in late December 2007. We submit that if Africa is able to seize the extraordinary period of growth that it is now enjoying, largely due to higher commodity prices, and use this time to invest in the development of its democratic institutions, that would do much to give lie to those who believe that initial conditions determine a country's destiny.

Africa, of course, possesses many if not all of the initial conditions that are held by economists to be most detrimental to sustained growth. Its natural environment gives rise to deadly diseases. The continent is relatively unfriendly to large-scale agriculture and the rearing of domestic animals (Diamond 2001). Several of its states are landlocked and most have commodity-based economies with little by way of a manufacturing base (a situation aided and abetted by industrial world tariff structures that discourage value-added investment). A crazy quilt of borders drawn by colonial administrators resulted in countries with high levels of ethnolinguistic fragmentation, and political competition based along these lines has engendered low levels of trust among peoples. In this setting, governments have traditionally been of the patrimonial type, with sharp distinctions drawn between "insiders" and "outsiders." And needless to add, during the eighteenth and nineteenth centuries many thousands of Africans were forced into slavery, with disastrous demographic and social consequences that reach into the present day. For all these reasons and many others, analysts have generally reached pessimistic conclusions regarding the region's prospects for sustained economic development, much less democratic consolidation.

Table 3.3 lists the African democratizers in our sample. The fact that over 63 percent of Africa's experiments with democracy ended in failure (compared with a failure rate of around 35 percent for the rest of the world) suggests that African democracies have indeed had a particularly difficult time achieving consolidation. In this chapter we highlight the particular role of ethnolinguistic fragmentation in causing particular difficulties for democratic consolidation, although other factors – like the presence of huge oil deposits in countries like Nigeria and Angola – could have also been emphasized.

With respect to this issue of ethnolinguistic divisions, it is certainly true that African democratizers have on average much higher levels of such fragmentation than their counterparts in other regions, as Figure 3.4 makes clear. Indeed, over 80 percent of Africa's young democracies have ethnic fragmentation that is higher than that of the world average – only 8 of the 44 African cases in our data set have below-average ethnic fragmentation. Of those cases with above-average ethnic fragmentation, the reversal rate for the 14 within one standard deviation of the mean was 42.8 percent, compared with a failure rate of nearly 74 percent for the 14 cases with fragmentation more than one standard deviation above the average. Thus, it would appear that democracy has indeed had more difficulty taking root in those African nations with very high ethnic fragmentation, as the Kenya case, with its sharp tribal divisions, makes clear.

In some respects, the themes that we have addressed in our discussion of Latin America resonate across the Atlantic in sub-Saharan Africa (hereafter referred to as SSA or simply Africa). African countries, like those in Latin America, are characterized by high levels of poverty and

TABLE 3.3. *Democratizations in sub-saharan Africa*

Country	Year of democratization	Year of reversal (if any)
Benin	1960	1963
Nigeria	1960	1964
Sierra Leone	1961	1967
Gambia	1965	1994
Equatorial Guinea	1968	1969
Sierra Leone	1968	1971
Ghana	1970	1972
Burkina Faso	1978	1980
Ghana	1979	1981
Nigeria	1979	1984
Benin	1991	
Mali	1992	
Niger	1992	1996
Ghana	1992	
Guinea-Bissau	1994	1998
Sierra Leone	1996	1997
Niger	1999	
Nigeria	1999	
Senegal	2000	
Ivory Coast	2000	2002
Congo Brazzaville	1960	1963
Congo Brazzaville	1992	1997
Central African Republic	1993	2003
Somalia	1960	1969
Uganda	1962	1966
Kenya	1963	1969
Sudan	1965	1969
Uganda	1980	1985
Sudan	1986	1989
Mozambique	1994	
Ethiopia	1995	
Djibouti	1999	
Kenya	2002	
Zambia	1964	1972
Lesotho	1966	1970
Botswana	1966	
Zimbabwe	1970	1987
Namibia	1990	
Zambia	1991	
Lesotho	1993	1998
Malawi	1994	
Mauritius	1968	
Comoros	1975	1976
Comoros	1990	1995
Madagascar	1992	
Comoros	2004	

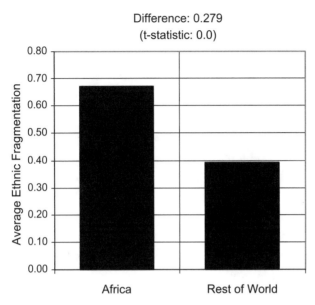

FIGURE 3.4. Ethnic Fragmentation in African Young Democracies.
Source: Alesina et al. (2003), Polity IV, authors' calculations.

inequality, which is particularly apparent among certain ethnic, linguistic, or geographic groups within nations, or what some have termed *horizontal inequality* (Stewart 2002). As in Latin America, these divisions have made it difficult for politicians to build broad bases of support, but whereas Latin leaders have employed populist tactics to build broad-based coalitions, politicians in Africa have generally resorted to targeting key supporters, often in the same ethnic group, and providing them with private goods or what is referred to as *clientelism.*

Keefer (2007a) shows that in many developing countries – including many young democracies in Africa – clientelism is the pervasive form of political organization, often grounded, for example, on ethnic ties between patron and client. This, too, becomes a default position when credibility is generally scarce; instead of seeking to build broad constituencies, politicians focus on the "in-groups," such as tribes, they already know. Thus, in such systems, the patrimonial leader does not seek to develop broad political support by providing voters with public goods like health care and education but instead maintains his position with the support of narrowly targeted groups who are rewarded with private goods like jobs and contracts. Keefer describes political clientelism in the following terms: "First, in clientelist countries, the credibility of political promises depends on a history of personal exchange and interaction between the promisor and the promisee. Second, patrons and clients have a preference for exchanges involving goods that benefit the recipient, narrowly, rather than a broader group" (Keefer 2007a).

When viewed as an imperfection in the political marketplace – meaning that a sharp distinction is drawn between insiders and outsiders, making it impossible to create, for example, broad-based, programmatic political parties – clientelism has far-reaching consequences for political and economic life in young democratic states (World Bank 2005). For example, if one of the benefits of democracy is found in its relatively generous provision of public goods – as a response to demands by voters – then clientelistic societies would skew these goods toward political insiders. As Keefer and Khemani have written, "Even in developing countries that are democracies, politicians often have incentives to divert resources to political rents and to private transfers that benefit a few citizens at the expense of many. *These distortions can be traced to imperfections in political markets that are greater in some countries than in others"* (Keefer and Khemani 2005; italics added).

Specifically, Keefer and Khemani explain that political market imperfections – including incomplete information, lack of credibility, and social polarization – can even lead to a distribution of so-called public goods that end up reaching only targeted groups rather than the population as a whole. As an illustration of the Keefer–Khemani thesis, consider the public goods of health care and education. The rate of infant mortality provides an important indicator of societal well-being (and, as our regressions report, is also associated with democratic reversal), and as societies become more developed, the rate of infant mortality tends to decline. But a simple cross-country correlation analysis between infant mortality rates on the one hand and ethnic fragmentation on the other demonstrates that the relationship is (weakly) positive: the higher the level of fragmentation in a society, the higher the level of infant mortality. Furthermore, fragmentation is also negatively related to the average levels of education in a given country (Kapstein 2004). These results would seem to support Keefer and Khemani's contentions regarding the availability of public goods in fragmented societies and suggest that democratization alone might not easily solve the problem posed by this "initial condition."

More generally, clientelistic systems engender uncertainty about whether property rights will be respected, particularly when one is an outsider (for more on this issue, see Kapstein 2004). As a consequence of this uncertainty, few productive investments are made, say, in agricultural land. In summary, socioeconomic as well as ethnic, linguistic, and geographic divisions constitute a challenging set of initial conditions that presumably hamper economic development to a significant extent.

But we follow Krieckhaus (2006) in suggesting that greater optimism may be warranted with respect to Africa in light of the region's recent experiences with democratization coupled with higher levels of growth. Overall, from an economic perspective, we find that Africa's young democracies have performed fairly well when compared to those in other regions and probably better than many people recognize. Their governments have contained inflation much more successfully than in Latin America or Eastern Europe and they have enjoyed relatively high levels of economic growth. For example, growth during the first five years following the democratizations in our data set is roughly the same for Africa and Latin America. The World Bank data show that during the period 2000–2005 growth in SSA averaged more than 3 percent per annum, higher than the levels achieved by Latin America (World Bank 2006). To be sure, this has been largely because of high commodity prices, and Africa certainly needs to prepare now for the end of this particular boom if growth is to be sustained. Africa has also benefited from the international community's Highly Indebted Poor Countries Initiative, which has relieved the continent of $35 billion in debt, along with the burdensome regular interest payments this entailed.

We confess that our cautiously optimistic view of Africa – the reasons for which we provide later – contrasts with those of many distinguished Africanists, who cast doubt on the capacity of democracy in the region to ameliorate the pernicious effects of challenging initial conditions or to avert bad economic outcomes like rampant corruption and rent-seeking. Noting the considerable variation in growth rates among states in the region, for example, Nicolas van de Walle has nonetheless concluded that "political liberalization has had little effect on economic performance in Africa" (van de Walle 1999, 22). Even earlier, Henry Bienen and Jeffrey Herbst had predicted that "the simultaneous pursuit of economic and political reform in Africa will be even more difficult than in most other regions of the world" (Bienen and Herbst 1996, 23).

As already noted, the reasons for this despair are based largely on Africa's initial conditions and particularly its patrimonial or clientelistic politics and high degree of ethnolinguistic fragmentation. If patrimonialism is primarily a response to ethnolinguistic fragmentation, and if such fragmentation is bad for economic performance, democratization would presumably have little effect on these underlying conditions and thus the associated outcomes. Further, given the fact that many African nations rely heavily on exports of commodities – petroleum, diamonds, coffee, and so forth – for their economic well-being, control over these items is heavily contested and tendencies to monopolize power are reinforced, further undermining democratic processes, broad-based economic development, and long-run growth.

It is not our place here to provide a complete, alternative picture of Africa's economic performance and its prospects for democratic consolidation. But we must stress that by any number of "human development" measures, life for most people in Africa has improved considerably over the past decades, despite the oft-discussed ravages of HIV/AIDS and other epidemics (Clemens, Kenny, and Moss 2004). Overall, life expectancies have jumped in the face of declining infant mortality levels; years of schooling have increased, including for girls; and the number of civil wars and ethnic conflicts has been falling, despite the atrocities in Darfur. Agriculture productivity has risen, as has the use of several technologies associated with economic growth, including computers and cell phones (Sender 1999). Of particular significance from our perspective, investment – including foreign direct investment – has risen significantly. Foreign investment, although still small, has tripled from the levels of the 1990s.

These changes raise the intriguing possibility that democracy, including the development of programmatic political parties that are now relatively strong in several countries (Carbone 2003), may have had a positive influence on the margins of African economic policy and performance by instilling some degree of transparency, accountability, contestation, and discipline in contemporary politics. By transparency we mean that more information is available about government decision-making and revenue use; by accountability we mean that politicians are increasingly called on to explain and justify their policies; by contestation we mean that political parties and a variety of interest groups are slowly organizing to challenge the domination of patrimonial leaders; and by discipline we mean that all these forces may be containing, if only to a small degree, the rent-seeking behavior of African elites. Furthermore, as Africa urbanizes, we would expect these trends to gain momentum, including the further development of political parties that seek to mobilize urban voters (Carbone 2003). Again, those who seek to help Africa's young democracies would do well to take note of such developments, in the process helping both political consolidation and long-run growth prospects. Unfortunately, as we show in Chapter 4, on foreign aid, we do not have much evidence that donors have necessarily drawn the right connections between political and economic development in the region.

To be sure, corruption is still widespread in Africa, at least judging from the rankings of agencies like Transparency International, and this undoubtedly discourages both foreign and domestic investment levels. Such high levels of corruption are endogenous to systems with insiders and outsiders, as the latter have to bribe the former if they are to receive any services at all. But for the first time in a long while, corruption has become a topic for public debate and judicial investigation. In South Africa, Nigeria, Zambia, and Kenya, the year 2006 saw a spate of government officials charged with corrupt practices. Although the practical effects of this new sensibility remain to be seen, at least the issue of corruption is now front and center in discussions of good governance.

The spread of democracy and party politics then may be limiting, at least in some countries, the worst abuses associated with super-presidentialism – long the prevalent institutional form in Africa – at least on the margins. Again, we recognize that this may be a rose-tinted picture of what is happening (all the more so as this is being written in the shadow of intertribal violence in Kenya), but we believe that democracy may have played some role in Africa's improved economic performance in a way that should not be overlooked or rejected. As a consequence, we would suggest that much more empirical research is needed into the relationship between democracy and economic performance in Africa.

Asia: Democratization in the Shadow of Authoritarian Success

With the military coups of 2006 in Thailand and in Fiji, the "soft coup" in Bangladesh in 2007, and the violence surrounding Pakistan's efforts to return to democracy in 2008, questions about the durability of democratic regimes in Asia are once again capturing public attention. Alongside any initial conditions that may make democratic consolidation especially difficult, Asia's new democracies must also contend with the widespread impression that authoritarian regimes have generally delivered strong economic performance in that part of the world while providing needed stability in their fractious polities. The conventional wisdom teaches that the economic miracle of the postwar era was led by the authoritarian "tigers" of East and Southeast Asia, while today communist China is one of the main locomotives driving the global economy. Indeed, some observers are speaking of a new "Beijing Consensus" that, they assert, "has begun to remake the whole landscape of international development" (Ramo 2004, 3).

Ironically, rather than contributing to the region's growth, the spread of democracy in Asia has been viewed by at least some scholars as possibly detracting from its generally outstanding performance. They believe that weak democracies are incapable of solving the region's underlying social problems, such as ethnic fragmentation and highly polarized polities that make it near impossible to assemble broad coalitions through "big tent," programmatic political parties (for a review, see Krieckhaus 2006). As the data suggest, both foreign and domestic investors much prefer authoritarian Singapore and communist China to the democratic Philippines or Indonesia, states in which young democracy has been oft-threatened by the military.

But if some authoritarian regimes in Asia have delivered the economic goods to their people, this is hardly the case everywhere even within the region, a point that has often been conveniently overlooked by analysts in discussions of Asia's political economy. The military leaders of Pakistan and Myanmar (Burma) have generally failed to deliver sustained growth, and, of course, regimes like that of the Khmer Rouge in Cambodia or the communists in Pyongyang were nothing short of disastrous on every level. Further, even in those countries where growth was strong, Asia's authoritarian leaders were often quite repressive, provoking a vicious political cycle in which social tensions could not easily be controlled without resorting to violence. For a variety of reasons, then, the impulse toward democratization has proven strong in Asia even in the context of tremendous economic success. If any region provides support to proponents of modernization theory – with their belief that democratic ideas and institutions can emerge only *after* a certain threshold level of income has been attained – then surely it must be East Asia.

However, it would only be fair to recognize that democracy has often been a mixed economic and political blessing for Asia, as such cases as Pakistan, Bangladesh, and the Philippines make clear. As a result, Asia today incorporates a large and diverse group of democratizers and democratization experiences. From the repeated democratic failures of Pakistan to the conflict-ridden nascent democracies of contemporary Afghanistan and Iraq to the consolidated democracies of modern South Korea and Taiwan, Asia provides a rich panorama – and any number of puzzles – for research into the sorts of political-economic issues that have been raised in this monograph.

In this section, we briefly treat what we see as two broad types of Asian young democracies: first, the "tigers," like South Korea and Taiwan, that seem to provide empirical support for economic modernization theory and, second, the "repeat democratizers," like Pakistan and Thailand, where democratic institutions have seemingly had difficulty taking root. We then turn to democratization in the "fragile states" of Afghanistan and Iraq.

We begin this section with a quick sketch of the experience of Asia's young democracies. Of the 23 democratizations that occurred in Asia between 1960 and 2004 (presented in Table 3.4), 13 or just over 52 percent were reversed, higher than the 40 percent reversal rate seen in our sample as a whole. This failure rate is second only to sub-Saharan Africa's 56 percent and notably higher than Latin America's (32 percent).

Although the average length of reversed democratization in Asia is 6.2 years, 64 percent of democratic episodes that were reversed ended within the first five years. Of note are Pakistan and Thailand, which are among the six countries in the sample to undergo four or more attempts at democratization, as well as Korea, which underwent three democratizations. In our sample, Pakistan is one of two countries that failed on their fourth attempt at democratization (the other is Peru; note that our sample does not include either the Thai coup of 2006 or the return to democracy in Thailand or in Pakistan in 2008).

TABLE 3.4. *Democratizations in Asia*[a]

Country	Year of democratization	Year of reversal (if any)
South Korea	1960	1961
South Korea	1963	1972
South Korea	1988	
Mongolia	1992	
Taiwan	1992	
Pakistan	1962	1971
Bangladesh	1972	1974
Pakistan	1973	1977
Pakistan	1988	1999
Nepal	1990	2002
Bangladesh	1991	
Thailand	1969	1971
Thailand	1974	1976
Thailand	1978	1991
Thailand	1992	
Cambodia	1993	1997
Fiji	1970	1987
Papua New Guinea	1975	
Solomon Islands	1978	2000
Philippines	1987	
Fiji	1990	
Indonesia	1999	
East Timor	2002	

[a] It might be argued that democracy in East Timor, Thailand, Fiji, and Bangladesh has now been reversed. Our data set ends in 2004, before these recent reversals.

Turning our attention to the economic performance of the Asian democratizers in our sample in Table 3.5, it is notable that economic collapse was most certainly *not* the cause of democratic reversal in most cases. In fact, the two cases with the highest initial growth were both reversed. In Thailand, growth during the brief democratic interlude of 1969–1970 averaged nine percent. Korea's nine-year democratic period from 1963 to 1971 likewise saw growth average over nine percent. Yet both these cases ended in reversal. *Indeed, one clear message from the Asian growth data is that high growth is not a guarantee that democracy will endure*, a theme we address in the following sections.

TABLE 3.5. *Growth and reversal in Asian young democracies*

	Sustained		Reversed	
	Country	Year of democratization	Country	Year of democratization
Low Initial[a] Growth	Papua New Guinea	1975	Bangladesh	1972
	Mongolia	1992		
	East Timor	2002		
High Initial[a] Growth	Philippines	1987	Pakistan	1962
	South Korea	1988	South Korea	1963
	Fiji	1990	Thailand	1969
	Bangladesh	1991	Fiji	1970
	Thailand	1992	Pakistan	1973
	Taiwan	1992	Thailand	1974
	Indonesia	1999	Thailand	1978
			Solomon Islands	1978
			Pakistan	1988
			Nepal	1990
			Cambodia	1993

[a] First five years, or if episode lasted less than five years, growth over the whole episode. Growth below the average for all young democracies classifed as low.

Economic Growth and Democracy in Asia

At the time of their most recent democratizations, both South Korea and Taiwan had become upper-middle-income countries, with per capita incomes of nearly $6,000 (in 2006 dollars). Scholars have used these examples to suggest the power of the economic modernization thesis: namely that once per capita income reaches a certain "threshold" level, demands for democracy become too strong for rulers to resist (Lee 2002), but where exactly this threshold lies remains open for debate.

Under what institutional conditions did sustained economic growth occur in the "tiger" economies? Analysts have "emphasized the strong role of the state in Taiwan and South Korea. In South Korea, the state played a crucial role in maintaining control over the business sector.... In Taiwan, the state maintained an active role to implement policies that channeled new techniques into productive investment, targeted key industries, and exposed these industries to international competition" (Bertrand 1998, 358). According to Robert Wade, it was no coincidence that strong authoritarian regimes were in power in these countries during their economic "take-off," because governments of this type were essential to controlling wage and consumption demands that could have derailed their growth project (Wade 1990).

If this conventional wisdom is correct, how can we reconcile the apparently strong performance of Asia's authoritarian regimes with the thesis that the system of checks and balances actually helps to stabilize young democratic regimes while contributing beneficially to their economic performance? Surprisingly, the evidence in fact confirms our view. As demonstrated in Table 3.6, all six cases in which constraints on the executive were weak ended in reversal.

We also observe a relationship between the level of ethnic fragmentation in Asian countries and the reversal of democracy (Table 3.7). In Asian countries with below-average ethnic fragmentation, democracy was sustained in 54.5 percent of cases, against only 22 percent of cases with above-average ethnic fragmentation, a substantial and statistically significant difference. Among the ethnically fragmented countries are Thailand and Pakistan, two of the countries in our data set that underwent four democratizations in their history (it is notable that of the six countries that experienced four or more democratizations – the others being Guatemala, Peru, Spain, and Greece – only Greece has low ethnic fragmentation); more on these later.

Overall, the results suggest a puzzle: namely "strong" presidential democracies may not consolidate even in cases where the authoritarian leaders who preceded them were economically successful. Whereas modernization theory posited a linear path to democracy via growth, the evidence makes us aware that the type of democracy once created is of tremendous importance to consolidation as well, irrespective of subsequent economic performance. That result is particularly telling in the case of two of Asia's repeat democratizers, Pakistan and Thailand.

TABLE 3.6. *Executive constraints and reversal in Asian young democracies*

	Sustained		Reversed	
	Country	Year of democratization	Country	Year of democratization
Weak[a] Executive Constraints			Pakistan	1962
			South Korea	1963
			Thailand	1969
			Thailand	1974
			Thailand	1978
			Cambodia	1993
Strong Executive Constraints	Papua New Guinea	1975	South Korea	1960
	Philippines	1987	Fiji	1970
	South Korea	1988	Bangladesh	1972
	Fiji	1990	Pakistan	1973
	Bangladesh	1991	Solomon Islands	1978
	Mongolia	1992	Pakistan	1988
	Taiwan	1992	Nepal	1990
	Thailand	1992		
	Indonesia	1999		
	East Timor	2002		

[a] "Weak" constraints received less than a 5 on Polity IV's scale of executive constraints.
Source: Polity IV, authors' calculations.

Asia's Repeat Democratizers

Pakistan has introduced democracy at least four times in its history: 1951, 1962, 1973, and 1988 (and again is attempting to do so in 2008). At the initiation of democratization in 1988, economic growth had been running around 6–7 percent per annum for over 10 years, and invest-ment levels had jumped by 50 percent, from 12 percent to 18 percent of GDP, during that time period. The economy was further bolstered by inflows of worker remittances and foreign aid; Pakistan in the late 1980s was a major recipient of official development assistance (Rais 1988).

TABLE 3.7. *Ethnic fragmentation and reversal*

	Sustained		Reversed	
	Country	Year of democratization	Country	Year of democratization
Below Ave.[a] Ethnic Fragmentation	Papua New Guinea	1975	South Korea	1960
	Philippines	1987	South Korea	1963
	South Korea	1988	Bangladesh	1972
	Bangladesh	1991	Solomon Islands	1978
	Mongolia	1992	Cambodia	1993
	Taiwan	1992		
Above Ave.[a] Ethnic Fragmentation	Fiji	1990	Pakistan	1962
	Thailand	1992	Thailand	1969
	Indonesia	1999	Fiji	1970
			Pakistan	1973
			Thailand	1974
			Thailand	1978
			Pakistan	1988
			Nepal	1990

[a] Refers to the average level of ethnic fragmentation in the full sample of young democracies. *Source:* Alesina et al. (2003), Polity IV, authors' calculations.

Despite these promising background conditions, Pakistan's last experience with democracy ultimately ended in a military coup led by General Pervez Musharraf in October 1999. Economic growth had collapsed with the return to democracy (there have always been questions about how democratic even elected Pakistani governments have been given the "feudal" system of land tenure and its consequences for voting behavior) and there were widespread allegations of corruption from both inside and outside the country. Transparency International rated Pakistan as among the most corrupt nations anywhere. Further, the administration of Benazir Bhutto and later that of Nawaz Sharif were blamed by many in Pakistan for allowing Islamic fundamentalism to threaten state institutions, including the army and the judicial system. In this context, at least, it is ironic that Bhutto's Pakistan Peoples Party and Sharif's

Pakistan Muslim League remain such major players in the country's politics. Overall, there was very little confidence in Pakistan's democratic institutions and their ability to deal with the nation's myriad challenges.

To be sure, by the late 1980s Pakistan had – at least by Polity measures – developed a relatively constrained executive (in this case meaning an elected prime minister who was subordinate to a president appointed by parliament) in that a system of checks and balances was in place. But it seems that democracy was so flawed in Pakistan – for example, only a small percentage of the citizenry actually voted for Sharif – that many doubted its institutional integrity from the outset.

Further, Pakistan was – and remains – a highly unequal country. Land holdings are highly concentrated and the educational system remains largely private and expensive, meaning access to it is reserved mainly for the children of the elite. Thus, there are very few channels open for social mobility. These conditions, combined with weak institutions, have made Pakistan's various democracies extremely fragile and prone to collapse during the nation's frequent political and economic crises; in fact, it is no exaggeration to say that crisis appears endogenous to the system, thus the frequent hope that the "man on horseback" will bring some stability.

What light does our research shed on Pakistan's failed attempts at democratization? We draw several conclusions. First, Pakistan has never fully developed the anatomy of democracy: the electoral mechanisms and institutions that give that system its popular legitimacy and leaders their credibility. Second, and related, the high levels of inequality and systemic failures to provide opportunities to all but a small group of persons means that a pool of citizens exists that is prepared to act either by "voting with their feet" and leaving the country – migrant remittances now constitute a crucial source of foreign exchange – or by rebelling from within (Tilly made this point about flawed democracies more generally; see Tilly 2007). Third, Pakistan's security environment – its "bad neighborhood" – gives the military a particularly strong role in society, one that is exceptional even by developing world standards. Finally,

Pakistan's fragmented society has not found internal means for reconciling differences in a way that would induce governments to generate public goods that benefit every citizen. Combined, these factors (undoubtedly among others we have not mentioned) have created a society that has been unable to generate either sustained growth or democratic consolidation.

Unfortunately, it does not seem that these shortcomings have been fully understood by those policy-makers and pundits who call so vociferously for a rapid return to democracy in Pakistan; indeed, it is unclear whether many of them are even aware of how many previous episodes of democratization Pakistan has experienced since becoming an independent state (see, for example, "Pakistani P.R.," *The New York Times,* February 1, 2008). This should not be taken to mean that we are opposed to the introduction of democracy in Pakistan, for that is hardly the case; instead, we would argue that some fundamental underlying conditions must be addressed within the country's political economy if democracy is likely to take root.

The other paradigmatic case of a repeat democratizer is Thailand, whose fourth experiment with democracy ended in a military coup in September 2006, only to launch a fifth episode 16 months later. Unfortunately, Thailand is among the small group of countries in our data set that started its various attempts at democratization with a compound set of difficult initial conditions: high inequality, high degrees of ethnic fragmentation, and low income. On top of these initial conditions, the various efforts at democratization were carried out in the context of strong presidential regimes with few checks and balances, and an absence of elite cohesion. As with most of our other cases that combined tough initial conditions with weak democratic institutions, Thailand's nascent democracies have proved unable to consolidate, and nonregime elites have balked at elected leaders, especially when those leaders use populist tactics as a way of gathering power.

Take Thailand's last case of democratization, launched in 1992 following the brief military coup that occurred the previous year. This time Thailand began with a much higher level of per capita income than before (over $1,700 in today's dollars – still below the amount that South Korea enjoyed when it embarked on the democratization process). Moreover, constitutional reforms initiated in the wake of the 1997 economic crisis provided for a much more vigorous set of checks and balances while strengthening the country's party system. But Thailand's young democracy was not yet consolidated and remained threatened by those elites who sought to capture state institutions for personal gain, and it collapsed following Prime Minister Thaksin's sale of his assets to Singapore-based Temasek holdings in 2006, confirming the skepticism on the part of some early analysts about the new constitution's durability (Case 2001).

Yet the overthrow of Thai democracy in 2006 nonetheless posed some significant puzzles. First, it occurred following a period of relatively strong economic growth; since 2000, economic growth had averaged five percent per annum; moreover, that growth had even reached poor, rural farmers, who saw their incomes rise during this time. The stock market was booming, strongly recovering from the financial crisis of 1997–1998. Thai democracy, then, was not reversed because of economic deterioration.

Second, the fourth round of Thai democracy (the various previous efforts were launched in 1969, 1974, and 1978) also had the added benefit of being introduced in the 1990s, a decade that has been generally supportive of the democratization experience, for reasons that are not altogether clear. As we have seen, far fewer newly democratic states that emerged in the 1990s have reversed than those started in earlier decades. Perhaps the combination of America's "unipolar power" and Washington's rhetorical preference for democracy, coupled with the globalization of capital and ideas, has made the recent era more conducive to nurturing young democracies.

Nonetheless, the Thai coup suggests that these forces have failed to "lock-in" democracy where domestic institutions are weak. It is telling that the latest constitution, sponsored by the military, again emphasizes efforts to check executive power, this time through the imposition of term limits (which are probably a good idea, though they can encourage short-term, rent-seeking maximization in societies where institutions that could monitor and punish such behavior are incapable of acting).

The cases of Pakistan and Thailand, then, demonstrate vividly many of the themes that we have raised in this monograph. Economic growth alone cannot rescue a democracy when institutions are weak, and finding ways of strengthening such institutions must be a crucial test for both domestic politicians and the international community that wishes to support them. As Pakistan and Thailand once again flirt with new rounds of democratization, the question of whether the right combination of formal and informal institutions finally exist, and are generally supported by those groups that could make or break the regime, must be at the forefront of policy analysis.

Democratization in Fragile States: Afghanistan and Iraq

It is not our objective in this book to discuss in any detail the special problems facing young democracies in "fragile states" or those in the midst of violent conflict. In many of these cases, including Afghanistan and Iraq, security issues remain so overwhelming as to trump any discussions of the relationship among political institutions, economic performance, and democratic consolidation. Clearly, levels of investment and the prospects for sustained growth will remain low in countries where the bullets are still flying and people are fearful of leaving their homes. Nonetheless, it is worth emphasizing that the international community – or at least the United States and several of its coalition partners – has seemingly taken the view that democracy must be established quickly even in these relatively hostile environments, and it is important to know why that might be the case. Further, it is important to know what *type* of democracy has arisen in these environments.

At the same time, policy-makers have often expressed the view that economies must get up and running as quickly as possible to create the background conditions against which peace might be established. In particular, it has long been held that widespread unemployment – especially among former servicemen – is particularly detrimental to conflict resolution. We are thus particularly interested in whether democracy as a regime type might favor economic recovery in these difficult environments.

It seems to us that the keys to this question might be found in such fundamental political economy concepts as legitimacy and credibility, concepts that we have evoked frequently in this book. That is, democracy as a regime type promises the legitimate representation of the interests of different groups within a society, while democratic institutions – including constitutional arrangements, elections, and political parties – are supposed to enhance the credibility of elected officials. These concepts, however, are not quickly or easily translated into political practice anywhere – this is why the age of democracy matters – and are all the more difficult to establish when any wellsprings of trust that may have existed within a society have been depleted by war and its aftermath.

Take the case of Iraq. There, advocates of a rapid democratization asserted that this government type could most quickly overcome the animosities that existed among the major groups in the country, specifically among Kurds, Shiites, and Sunnis (Byman and Pollack 2003). By creating representation that was primarily *geographical* as opposed to ethnic in origin, by creating strong regional governments, and by creating a constrained executive with effective checks and balances, at least some analysts felt that Iraqis would "have an incentive to find compromise solutions to national problems..." (Byman and Pollack 2003, 128). In short, by establishing a legitimate government that effectively gave voice to Iraq's different interest groups while providing incentives for them (e.g., a share in the country's future oil rents) to engage in peaceful bargaining over public policy, a democratic Iraq could achieve stability and set itself on the path to economic growth.

What these analysts overlooked, however, was the intensity with which the losers from the war – that is, the Sunnis – would fight to maintain their privileged position or else take the entire country down with them. This response is suggestive of the democratization model posited by Acemoglu and Robinson (2006) in which they argued that democracy was unlikely to take root in societies where preexisting inequalities were too great. In these cases, the elite simply had no interest in democratization, which must lead to significant asset losses on their part. Thus, for the Sunnis, democratization simply represents a method for ridding them of their privileged position, and so the benefits of fighting outweigh the costs of accepting a democratic regime.

That has also been the case to some degree in Afghanistan, where the Taliban have continued their war against the government in Kabul and the coalition forces stationed in the country. But unlike in Iraq, the coalition appears to have an objective of defeating and destroying the opposition – in this case, the Taliban – at least as an effective military force (but even in Afghanistan, where military operations have widespread rhetorical support from the international community, we note that troop levels have also been far short of what the generals claim are needed to defeat the enemy). In short, where opponents of the regime cannot be easily co-opted – and it seems that the United States severely underestimated its ability to co-opt or defeat the Sunnis in Iraq – they must be eliminated as direct threats if a young democracy is to stabilize.

Yet there are further lessons to be drawn from Iraq and Afghanistan with respect to the relationship between democracy and economic performance. Presumably, the ongoing commitment of the world's democracies – again, led by the United States – to these nations is greatly enhanced to the extent they are viewed as members of the democratic family of nations. In an important sense, this family provides some degree of "lock-in" in the absence of stronger international or regional arrangements like the European Union. The international community, in turn, is supposed to enhance these democracies' chances for survival by providing them with foreign aid and technical assistance, not to mention security. In short, by being democratic they will receive the assistance that will help their economies grow, in turn consolidating the democratic regime. Again, in practice, the ability of the international community to deliver on this promise, such as it is, has been disappointing. In Iraq, for example, electricity blackouts and water shortages remain common, despite billions of dollars in aid that were allegedly targeted at these very infrastructure problems and shortfalls (James Glanz, "In Iraq, A Failure to Deliver the Spoils," *New York Times*, August 13, 2006).

Overall, then, it seems that the theory underlying democratization in fragile states is that this regime type is most likely to deliver legitimacy and credibility to war-torn settings. At the same time, these young democracies are more likely than authoritarian regimes to receive assistance from the international community. At least in Iraq and Afghanistan, these theoretical propositions seem very far from the reality "on the ground." How to establish legitimacy and credibility are among the greatest questions facing scholars of modern political economy, and finding answers is obviously a pressing issue for public policy as well (Keefer 2007a).

Despite the obvious challenges facing governmental institutions in Afghanistan and Iraq, we nonetheless believe that the type of democratic institutions that are being created there – which have sought to disperse power – are appropriate and will ultimately serve these countries well, when (assuming that day eventually arrives) their internal violent conflicts give way to political negotiation. This view, we emphasize, is in contrast to that of some observers who argued that both Afghanistan and Iraq needed "strong" governments with powerful executives, who could ride roughshod over their political opponents. Thus, we agree with Byman and Pollack, who asserted as early as 2003 that "the key for an Iraqi democracy will be to fashion a system that addresses the potential problem of the tyranny of the majority," in this case the Shiite community (Byman and Pollack 2003, 127). They recommended as a consequence a regime type in which power was shared across regions, ethnic groups, and legislative bodies.

We note in closing that Iraq, even more than Afghanistan, enters its democratic experiment with some powerful advantages. It has an educated and entrepreneurial population, and its oil reserves – which are a double-edge sword for a democracy, as they induce rent-seeking behavior – could provide a reliable source of national income to pay for needed public goods. Indeed, when looked upon through the lens of modernization theory, few Arab countries would seem more primed for democracy than Iraq.

Yet as we have seen, modernization theory's predictive power has proved limited. Today, the main challenge in both Afghanistan and Iraq is to provide security, enabling the citizens of those countries to get on with their lives. Only then can debates over how to consolidate these fragile democracies have any substantive meaning.

Conclusions

Why do economic policies and political outcomes differ so much across the world's young democracies? Clearly, initial conditions make a difference. Oil-rich and ethnically fragmented countries are less likely to be democratic or to remain so, whereas governments facing high levels of income and asset inequality may be tempted to pursue short-run fixes that are destabilizing over the long run.

But initial conditions do not determine a country's destiny once and for all. If they did, how would we explain the success of many "repeat democratizers" in consolidating their regimes, including several countries that have labored under a battery of initial conditions that are held to be inimical to political and economic development? Clearly, the institutions that leaders build and the policy choices they make matter to prosperity and stability as well.

In particular, following Fish (2001) and Weyland (2002, 2003), we have suggested that both economic reform and democratic governance tend to be weakest in those countries that have adopted "super-presidential" systems of power – systems found in countries spread from Latin America to the former Soviet Union. Ironically, these systems came to power at least in part on the back of a promise that strong presidents were best suited to rolling up their sleeves and administering the bitter medicine of reform to reluctant populations. Instead, the concentration of economic and political power stifled both development and consolidation and played to the hands of the "insiders" who supported the chief executive.

Although this finding resonates with those who argue that parliamentary regimes tend to do the best job of checking the abusive power of the president, especially in developing countries where legislative bodies and political parties tend to be weak, it is important to bear in mind our finding, discussed in earlier chapters, that parliamentary democracy does not provide a sturdy bulwark against reversal. More than regime type, what matters is the effectiveness of checks and balances, which are undoubtedly a product of both formal institutions and the informal organizations of civil society. Building these institutions, including programmatic political parties, appears to be crucial to the process of democratic consolidation.

Our analysis thus supports the view of Satyanath and Subramanian (2004) that the quality of democratic institutions matters greatly to economic performance, and in particular to the dampening of economic volatility. In their study of cross-national variations in macroeconomic stability, for example, they find that "a one standard deviation improvement in democracy leads to a 3.6 fold decline in nominal instability in particular." In particular, they argue that "greater checks and greater accountability should be associated with greater macroeconomic stability" and then go on to suggest that "democracies are likely to be more macro-economically stable."

At the same time, we have shown that it is misguided to hope that young democracies will necessarily spawn institutional developments of the kind that promote macroeconomic stability in particular and the context for sustained economic growth and democratic consolidation more generally. That depends on the extent to which local conditions – not to mention the international community – favor strong presidents and populist or clientelistic policies, to the exclusion of "independent" institutions. When governments make choices about the political and economic rules of the game, some combination of domestic and foreign actors must be present to ensure that these rules are inclusive and broad based, encouraging competition rather than crushing it. It is because of the central importance of the political and economic diffusion of power to democracy that helps to explain why the Polity measures that we use emphasize the constraints placed on the executive power, a fact that has also been commented on by Beck and Laeven (2005).

In short, whether democracies reverse or consolidate is not simply a function of economic performance, as much of the academic literature has long reported. Perhaps even more critically, it is a function of whether societies, especially societies where initial conditions seem unfavorable to development, are able to craft governance arrangements that are characterized by effective checks and balances. To put this in other words, difficult initial conditions can be mitigated by political choices that give people confidence in the new regime type, and this seems to be happening to some extent in perhaps the "hardest cases" for democratic consolidation around, namely the countries of SSA. Indeed, the consolidation of democracy in SSA would make life very difficult for those who expound the "initial conditions" thesis. But domestic choices alone may not be sufficient. The international community can also play a potentially decisive role in democratic consolidation, particularly where policy capabilities and resources are in short supply. We pursue that issue in the next chapter.

4 Is Democracy Promotion Effective?

Democracy programs frequently treat the symptoms rather than the causes of democratic deficits.

Thomas Carothers (1999)

WE BELIEVE THAT THE FINDINGS PRESENTED IN THIS book have potentially important consequences for industrial world's foreign assistance policies and programs that have democracy promotion as one of their key objectives. Specifically, we have argued that the leaders of young democracies may face great challenges in establishing their legitimacy and credibility, especially in divided societies where trust among social groups is lacking. In such cases, leaders may try to concentrate power by pursuing policies that enrich particular, targeted groups of "insiders" over the short run, but at the cost of undermining the broader public's faith in the value of democratic institutions. When weak political institutions combine with poor economic performance, democracy is unlikely to take root; in fact, when the institutions of newly democratic states are of poor quality, even relatively strong growth may not save them from backsliding or reversal, as so many recent cases (e.g., Thailand, Venezuela, and Russia) unfortunately illustrate.

Further, we have seen that the *kind* of economic performance may also matter to democratic consolidation. If countries enjoy growth but the wealth is not spread equitably, or in a way that promotes opportunities for socioeconomic mobility, consolidation may prove more difficult to achieve; as we have already seen in Chapter 2, highly unequal countries are less likely to remain democratic. We thus concur with Larry Diamond, who has written, "If growth is distributed reasonably well and inflation is restrained, all classes gain a stake in the system, confident that democracy can work for them, and the range of ideological and political differences is lessened" (Diamond 1999, 88).

If both the design of political institutions and the pattern of economic growth and income and asset distribution are critical to democratic consolidation, what are the implications for foreign assistance? In recent years, the industrial world's foreign aid programs – and our focus here is on the programs of the United States, although we believe that our generalization holds true across most European Union aid programs as well – have seemingly adopted a "two-track" approach to democratic consolidation, with one track emphasizing political institutions and a separate track devoted to fostering economic growth (this division, of course, greatly simplifies the reality of the matter as foreign assistance serves a multitude of objectives, from military and security assistance to combating the scourge of infectious diseases like HIV/AIDS).[1] It is the major contention of this chapter that such a division should be revisited in that effective, credible institutions that serve to diffuse political and economic power are crucial for *both* democratic consolidation and sustained economic development.

Further, economic policy – *including particularly a concern with redistribution broadly defined* – must be designed in such a way as to support the process of democratic consolidation (World Bank 2006). *In an important sense, the redistribution of incomes, assets, and opportunities is the economic corollary of political checks and balances in that both serve to block extreme concentrations of power by encouraging pluralization.*

---

[1] When we made this statement about the division of aid to U.S. officials, we expected them to reply that, in practice, there was substantial policy coordination among the different units; in fact, what we heard is that "the situation is even worse than you can imagine!"

Thus, one focus of democracy-promoting foreign aid must be to encourage new economic agents to enter the domestic and global marketplaces; in fact, this is yet another reason why industrial countries should open their markets to developing world exports and why protectionism, by stifling entrepreneurship in young democracies, can have dire economic *and* political consequences.

We are thus concerned in what follows with how the democratization agenda can be most effectively promoted by the foreign assistance community through a tighter integration of institution building and economic reform. To preview our analysis, we believe that the "country compact" approach adopted by the new Millennium Challenge Corporation (MCC) comes closest to the sort of foreign assistance program that could serve the twin objectives of advancing democracy and generating development dividends. The MCC's approach of targeting reforms like land titling alongside the building of complementary institutions like independent judiciaries holds the potential of winning broad public support. *Such programs, however, must be carefully designed if they are not to be captured by those local elites who would use them to advance their own narrow interests at the expense of the country's democratic project.*

We would also make one additional point at the outset. If our data show anything, it is that young democracies are particularly vulnerable to reversal during their first five years of existence. This indicates that the international community must provide comprehensive support to the world's young democracies to ensure that they get "over the hump" of those early years: that they successfully confront and manage the early challenges to democratic consolidation that will surely come their way. Unfortunately, we do not believe that the international community has always been willing to provide such support, as the attention spans of elected officials are short and there are always new crises – foreign and domestic – to meet. The shift of foreign assistance attention and resources – including military resources – from Afghanistan to Iraq, for example, has arguably had powerful and largely negative consequences for the former at a particularly crucial juncture in its democratic evolution.

We begin this chapter by briefly reviewing the evidence on whether foreign aid has been effective in supporting democratization and democratic consolidation in the past. We then turn to the MCC and a discussion of its policies, with a focus on land titling reform. We conclude with some suggestions for policy and for research.

Does Foreign Aid Promote Democracy?

As noted in the introduction to this volume, recent years have seen a dramatic shift in development thought and policy-making: today it is widely believed that democracy is *necessary* for both sustained growth and political stability. In this context it should be remembered that, for most of the postwar era, the relationship between democracy and development was shaped by "modernization theory," in which democracy was viewed instead as an outgrowth or result of the development process. In short, modernization theory has been turned on its head by contemporary policy-makers in the aid community.

Why did that transformation occur? Carothers reports that events in many poor countries during the 1960s led foreign aid officials to question the tenets of modernization theory and the inevitable connection they (and many academics) once drew between growth and democracy. He writes that their "shining hopes... had not been realized. Despite unprecedented amounts of aid, poverty and misery were still rife in the developing world. Moreover, what economic growth had occurred had not produced the expected payoff in politics. If anything, democracy had retreated... " (Carothers 1999, 27).

This loss of confidence in modernization theory helped shape the realist or strategic foreign aid policies of the Nixon era, with their emphasis on strengthening politico-military ties with recipient – particularly anti-communist – governments, no matter their regime type. In pendulum fashion, these strategic aid policies then gave way during the

Carter Administration to an emphasis on using aid to bolster human rights (indeed, Jimmy Carter's own moral predilections were bolstered by widespread media coverage of human rights abuses in several recipient nations of U.S. aid, mainly in Latin America). By the 1980s, President Ronald Reagan's frontal assault on the communist world would include a strong dose of active "democracy promotion," which became an explicit foreign assistance objective of the United States. Since then, it has evolved into what Carothers calls a "core priority" of foreign aid, and funding for it has nearly doubled over the past five years, rising from $560 million in 2001 to $1 billion in 2006 (Carothers 1999, 29ff; Finkel, Perez-Linan, and Seligson 2006). As Carol Lancaster has nicely put it, "foreign aid began as one thing and became another" (Lancaster 2007).

The history of aid naturally raises the questions of how foreign assistance has been used to promote democratization and democratic consolidation in recent years, whether such assistance has been effective in advancing those objectives, and what if any changes in assistance policies and allocations might be appropriate in the interest of supporting the world's young democratizers. For example, do regimes that "rule justly" make better use of foreign aid in terms of providing public goods and/or balancing their budgets? If so, should some "initial" level of democracy be a precondition of receiving foreign aid in the first place?

While seeking to answer these questions, we recognize that many scholars, activists, and even policy-makers have already reached their own conclusion that aid can never usefully serve the "democracy and development" agenda, no matter how wisely the money is allocated. For these critics, aid undermines both democracy and development by rewarding the few who are in power and by centralizing their economic and political authority. Like oil, aid can become a kind of "curse" to its recipients, impeding democracy and development rather than promoting these objectives. Still, it must be recognized that the international community has undoubtedly played a useful role in helping to "lock-in" democratic reforms in many countries, especially by incorporating young democracies within such regional groupings as the European Union or within international institutions like the World Trade Organization. As Carothers puts it, "Democracy aid was not the driver of the 'third wave' of democratization, but it was a useful partner in the process" (Carothers 2007, 113).

Further, aid might make a crucial difference to cash-strapped, post-conflict regimes that appear devoted to doing the right thing, like putting into place needed economic and institutional reforms, as in the case of contemporary Liberia and its dynamic leader Ellen Sirleaf Johnson. Indeed, we showed in our regression analysis that aid does seem to increase the likelihood that a young democracy will survive. More pragmatically, in this chapter we simply accept that foreign aid is and will remain part of the international community's efforts to help these nations and we try to suggest some ways in which such aid can be made more effective.

If aid is to have its maximum impact on growth and democracy, policy-makers will require some clear decision-rules about when, where, and how it should be allocated. One decision-rule might be to give aid only to countries that are already democratic or, in the phrase of the MCC (more on this institution in the following section), "rule justly." But do democracies in fact make better use of foreign aid than authoritarian regimes? And is there any evidence that foreign aid can actually promote democracy in the first place?

Turning to the first question, Svensson (1999) found in an oft-cited study that aid has a much larger effect on income growth in democratic versus nondemocratic nations. He posits that "since foreign aid is intermediated by the recipient government, a study of the macroeconomic impact of aid needs to include a realistic model of government behavior" (Svensson 1999, 275). In particular, he argues that the *checks and balances* implicit in democratic governance will place some controls on the government's use of foreign aid funds, limiting opportunities for kleptocratic behavior. That is an argument we are sympathetic toward and that may be true *on average* – and recall that regression analysis often presents its results in such terms – but as we have seen, "democracy" alone provides no guarantee that limits will be placed on strong executives. Instead, this is an institutional variable among democracies that needs to be manipulated in the interest of pluralizing power, and how and why elites agree to such an arrangement is perhaps one of the great questions for democratic theory (Huntington 1991; Tilly 2007). We will discuss it in greater detail in the following chapter.

With respect to the question of whether aid can serve to promote a country's democratization process, the jury still remains out. In one of the earliest studies of its kind, the World Bank's Steven Knack found that foreign assistance does not seem to result in more democracy. Knack, however, did not attempt to disaggregate aid spending into its constituent parts; that is, he did not isolate any independent effects of democracy promotion funds for elections, state institutions, and civil society on democratic outcomes. In support of classic modernization theory, however, he found that economic growth contributes positively to higher levels of democracy, with the finding strongest for Latin America and Eastern Europe and weaker for Africa (Knack 2000).

A recent study sponsored by the United States Agency for International Development (USAID), in contrast, has tried to assess the independent effects of U.S. democracy promotion funds – that is, funds specifically targeted at elections, state institutions, and civil society – on the growth of democracy around the world. The authors find that foreign aid used for these purposes has had "a significant positive impact on democracy, while all other U.S. and non-U.S. assistance variables" – including aid which is targeted at economic growth – "are statistically insignificant." Specifically, "for every 10 million additional dollars of U.S. democracy assistance, a country is predicted to be .25 units, or one-quarter of a point higher on the Freedom House general democracy index in a given year" (Finkel, Perez-Linan, and Seligson 2006, 53).

Again, we emphasize the finding of this study *that aid granted for any purpose other than democracy promotion assistance is not significantly associated with an increase in a country's level of democracy.* Thus, aid spent on economic growth does *not* seem to have even an indirect effect on levels of democratization. Consequently, this suggests that if aid that is oriented toward economic reform and growth is also meant to foster democracy, even by indirect channels, then policy-makers will have to give much deeper thought to the connections that run between economics and democratization, as they appear to be far from mechanical.

One powerful belief that seems to inform the aid community is that once a democracy is in place, economic success will bolster popular support for the regime and help lead to its consolidation. Following this line of reasoning, pro-growth assistance programs can foster democratization by helping to deliver a "democracy dividend." That is, citizens will come to draw a causal connection between the regime type and their economic well-being. *Our research, however, suggests this is not in fact the case. We showed in the previous chapter that improved economic performance in terms of GDP growth alone does not ensure the survival of the newly established democratic government.* Instead, we believe that both economic aid and democracy promotion assistance must be targeted in such a way as to encourage the pluralization of economic and political power. This means that economic policies must encourage some promise of redistribution, at least of opportunities if not of income and assets, for which policy support, at least in the West, seems to have diminished (see also Tilly 2007 for an elaboration of this point). In this context, however, we are reminded that income and asset redistribution (particularly land reform) were once quite central objectives of U.S. aid policy (and perhaps that of the World Bank as well – think of its classic book of 1974 entitled *Redistribution with Growth*); today, as we will see later, the emphasis has changed somewhat and now land *tenure* as opposed to land *reform* has emerged as a major aid target.

Interestingly from our perspective, Finkel and colleagues also found that "the impact of AID Democracy and Governance (DG) obligations appears to differ somewhat across regional contexts. The effect of DG assistance is strongest in Asia, with African countries also exhibiting DG impacts that are substantially greater than those seen for the baseline regions. The size of the coefficients for Asia and Africa indicates that the effect of DG obligations increases roughly by a factor of two in those regions. The DG effect for Latin America is somewhat lower..." (2006, 80). The fact that democracy assistance has very different regional effects, if that is indeed the case, is worthy of substantially more research and also lends support to the need for understanding regional variations in democratic performance more generally, as indicated in the previous chapter.

In short, the message that we draw from the academic literature on foreign aid and democracy, together with our own research, is that international support for young democracies is likely to be most effective when economic and political assistance are deployed in a coherent fashion to support economic and political pluralization, taking into account the distinctiveness of each country setting. For example, foreign aid that strengthens the executive branch of government *at the expense* of other branches of government, or that provides private benefits to one group in particular at the expense of civil society more broadly, can undermine the prospects for consolidation over the long run. But the crucial question is this: what would a coherent set of policies look like? One interesting model that aims at some semblance of policy coherence with respect to the democracy and development agenda while seemingly avoiding "cookie-cutter" approaches to assistance is provided by the U.S. government's newest aid program, the MCC, which we examine in the following section.

Promoting Democracy and Development: The Millennium Challenge Corporation

President George W. Bush launched the MCC in 2002 to provide aid to low-income countries that were "ruling justly, investing in their people,

and encouraging economic freedom" (cited in Radelet 2003, 1). In part-
nership with these countries, the MCC has offered assistance that is
explicitly targeted at economic growth and poverty reduction, the underlying idea being that such growth will bolster these fledgling democratic
regimes. Unlike USAID, therefore, the MCC has an *explicit* "democracy
and development" agenda.

The MCC uses six indicators that seek to measure "just and democratic governance," including a country's demonstrated commitment to
"promote political pluralism, equality, and the rule of law; respect human
and civil rights, including the rights of people with disabilities; protect private property rights; encourage transparency and accountability
of government, and combat corruption" the (MCC, *Indicator Descrip-
tions*, at www.mcc.gov; see also the discussion in Radelet 2003). With
respect to political and civil liberties, MCC makes use of the Freedom
House (rather than Polity) scores, which rank countries on a scale from
1 to 7 (*most free* to *least free*). Many of the other political indicators
are drawn from the World Bank's governance index, also known as
the "Kaufmann–Kraay Governance Indicators" (www.worldbank.org).
Recent years have seen some controversy over the extent to which the
MCC actually relies on these indicators in making its decisions in practice, and Freedom House in particular would like to see a stronger commitment from the MCC in ensuring that only states deemed democratic
are made eligible to receive assistance.

Regional factors also appear to have some influence on MCC's allocation of scarce resources. Interestingly, of the 23 countries that are eligible to receive MCC funding as of late 2006, it is notable that 14 of
them are in Africa; the remaining 9 are evenly distributed with 3 each
from Latin America, Eurasia, and Asia. This seems to indicate a belief
among MCC officials that their "country compacts" – that is, their bilateral agreements with recipient nations – will have their largest multiplier
effects within the context of Africa's nascent democracies, a belief that
garners empirical support from Finkel, Perez-Linan, and Seligson (2006),
as reported in the previous section.

What forms of MCC assistance are most likely to bolster the world's young, democratic regimes? One cannot read the MCC's country compacts without detecting that the economic programs it supports have a decidedly redistributive, pluralistic, and "democratic ring" to them. Indeed, one cannot review the contents of the compacts without thinking that the MCC has been strongly influenced by the writings of Hernando De Soto and Douglass North if not Thomas Jefferson (North 1990; De Soto 2003). The MCC therefore seems to place a particularly strong emphasis on land tenure and titling as the basis for sustained growth in predominantly rural societies. Those small holders, in turn, seemingly form the backbone of a democratic polity in which power and decision-making are decentralized.

By promoting land titling, in turn, both the economy and democratic polity are strengthened. This general idea, incidentally, is hardly new in U.S. foreign policy; in fact, as already noted, the United States has long urged developing nations to undertake land reform and pressed such policies on governments from South America to South Asia (Russett 1964). The difficulty of advancing politically feasible redistribution policies, however, has perhaps cooled Washington's ardor for that approach and shifted its focus from reform to titling as another path toward the same end. Unfortunately, we remain skeptical of how much faith should be placed in the titling nostrum, especially in countries where elites are prepared to exploit the titling process for personal gain.

This is not to deny the potential importance of titling and the possibility that it can serve as the basis for important economic and political changes. In its country compact with Madagascar, for example, the MCC will provide support to reform "a poorly-functioning financial system that fails to serve the rural poor and a weak land-titling system that fails to provide legally-recognized collateral to support credit and investments in poor rural areas" (MCC, Compact with Madagascar, 27 April 2005, at www.mcc.org). The latter, again, reminds us of De Soto's fierce defense of the primordial importance of land titling for the poor (De Soto 2003), whereas the former – financial market deepening – points to one of the keys to social mobility in democratic societies: access to capital (Landa and Kapstein 2001). Clearly, establishing clearer property rights and promoting financial deepening are both crucial tasks for developing nations.

Similarly, in Benin, the MCC's compact focuses on creating "secure land tenure for the poor... and to create effective, transparent governance of land and property issues" while also expanding "the financial services available to micro, small and medium-sized enterprises... " (MCC, Compact with Benin, at www.mcc.org). To be sure, land titling is hardly the same thing as land redistribution (although the two could be related to the extent that customary users of land receive legal title to the land they occupy and/or farm), but it is still an important step in securing the property rights that can serve as the basis for asset collateral; asset collateral that can then be used to help finance a family's various projects, including putting children through school. However, we again note that empirical research does not provide strong support for the linkage between land titling and access to credit, since it is hard for lenders, practically speaking, to seize people's land holdings (See Galiani and Schargrodsky 2006).

In fact, if modern political economy can be said to have contributed anything to contemporary development theory and policy, it is the insistence on the importance for long-run growth of institutions that promote and protect property rights (North 1990). The reasoning is straightforward: growth requires investment, and investment will not occur when people are fearful of their property rights. The World Bank claims: "The benefits of secure tenure for households are well known. They include higher productivity, greater access to credit, higher propensity to invest in physical assets and the education of children" (World Bank 2006). From a macro perspective, the relationship between secure property rights and economic growth appears strongly established, even though the causality remains contested, and, in fact, the two could be simultaneously explained by some omitted third variable (for a literature review see Keefer 2004).

But one problem for both local leaders and for the foreign assistance specialists who wish to help them is that launching economic reforms such as the provision of land tenure may be easier than building durable institutions, like independent judiciaries, which help "lock-in" the benefits of the reform process. Thus, while advocating greater land tenure security through titling may help create the small farmers who provide, in Jeffersonian fashion, crucial political support to nascent democratic regimes, the real security of such property rights will ultimately depend on whether judiciaries and enforcement agencies are capable of instilling law and order. Beyond security, farmers will also need the support of complementary institutions like capital markets to obtain the credit needed for fertilizer and other inputs that increase agricultural productivity (but for skeptical views see Field and Torero 2006 and Galiani and Schargrodsky 2006). Again, we will see that the MCC has seemingly recognized this interaction between democracy and potentially redistributive policies like land tenure reform and titling to a large extent, although it may have the causal chain backward. *Thus, it may not be property rights that induce a demand for greater democracy but rather democracy that generates stronger property rights institutions* (Gradstein 2005).

But is land titling really an effective institutional mechanism for advancing the democratization and development agenda, as so much economic research would have us believe? The answer does not seem to be straightforward, and the insistence on land titling could reflect the interests of those who are most powerful in developing world societies rather than the poor (in this context it is interesting to note that the Pilgrim settlers of Plymouth Plantation during the early seventeenth century insisted on establishing land titling among the local Indian tribes so they could "buy" the land "legitimately" from tribal chiefs). As a University of Wisconsin report states,

> individualization through titling and registration has the potential to incite greater insecurity for the majority of rural populations by providing opportunities for those with greater wealth or status to acquire rights at the expense of the poor, whether it be wealthy government officials over smallholder farmers, landowners over borrowers, or men over women ... Where land speculation

exists as a primary motive encouraging those registering rights to resources...agricultural production is most likely to suffer. (Bruce 1996)

In short, land titling promises to advance two economic objectives in theory – security and efficiency – but whether it delivers them in reality on the ground is an empirical question about which little is known; so far as we are aware, studies of that question are limited. A recent World Bank analysis of Ghana finds that customary patterns of land use undermine efficiency-enhancing investments, particularly fallowing, by inducing farmers to exhaust the land rather than let it lie unseeded for fear it will be taken from them. But Goldstein and Udry (2005) admit that "long-term panel data" on the broader effects of formal titling arrangements on land allocation are limited. This, it seems to us, is a key question that must be studied in further detail before too much weight is placed on titling as a "democracy and development" policy.

It is interesting to note that land tenure reform has emerged as a major issue in African politics alongside the recent democratization movements of the 1990s. As noted earlier, one might think of this connection as a "natural" one, but the Wisconsin report tellingly warns that

Political democratization is not necessarily promoted by the individualization of tenure rights. Yet one senses that the Jeffersonian idea of widely distributed private property rights among a solid, roughly egalitarian class of small to medium landholders underlies some of the recent policy toward registration and titling of holdings in some country. The theorized link between private property and democracy has been an important element of Western political philosophy for centuries and is not without influence in policy debates and formulation in non-Western parts of the world. The logic is that individual or local ownership, or at least some element of local control or authority regarding land and natural resources, facilitates participation in the democratic process by increasing one's stake in the process. Democracy, in turn, is thought to facilitate tenure security through the efforts of its practitioners: landholders...The theorized link between private holdings or decentralized authority and democracy does not necessarily translate into workable institutions... (Bruce 1996, 14).

The problem, according to the Wisconsin researchers, is as follows:

Individualization initiatives that encourage land registration and titling programs may not be democratic in the sense of allowing fair and equal access to the registration process. In Benin [an MCC compact country], for example, minority groups such as serfs and ex-slaves may lose tenure access rights as landowners solidify their control over the natural resource base. *If democratization is a national priority, disadvantaged groups and social classes must not be excluded from or by individualization initiatives* (Bruce 1996, 15; italics added).

The crucial point worth repeating is that although the MCC may be right in drawing a connection between land titling, economic growth, and democracy, it may have the causal chain backward. Disagreeing with North, De Soto, and much of the received literature, Gradstein (2005) argues that it is democratization that promotes property rights and not vice versa. Rather than hope that land titling will induce a greater demand for democracy, one instead could emphasize the need for unbiased institutions that work on behalf of all citizens if property rights are to be truly protected and if land titling is to serve as a means for ensuring the poor's access to land. It is democratization, including, of course, the diffusion of political power, that provides the best guarantee against clientelism and kleptocracy; again, land titling without supporting democratic institutions could just become a land grab, as privatization through vouchers became an industrial grab in Russia during the early years of transition.

What all this suggests is that although land titling may be an appropriate means of advancing the democracy with growth agenda, the linkage may not be as tight as some would like to think, at least in terms of property rights leading to democratization. If land titling is to ensure the security of those who currently farm the land, including those who are least advantaged, special efforts will be needed to ensure that their interests are respected in the titling process. To be sure, titling is necessary, but not sufficient, for providing a pathway by which small landholders can gain access to credit, enabling them to become more productive while meeting other family needs. But if it becomes a mechanism by which the wealthy dispossess the poor, then land titling will have proved just another failed social experiment, and democratic institutions will remain weak.

Despite these words of caution about the MCC's focus on land titling (among other economic reforms it had advanced through its programs), it is nonetheless our view that the MCC is making a distinctive effort to advance at least an implicit "democracy and development" agenda, as reflected by its concern with potentially powerful redistributive measures as land titling, access to credit, and the strengthening of judicial systems. That means that would-be democracy promoters should pay special attention to its policies and programs. The idea that animates the MCC is, in our view, an excellent one that deserves widespread support; young democracies should receive special assistance from the world's advanced industrial countries and be given the opportunity to grow and to consolidate. Of course, this also requires a battery of other complementary policies in the West, including greater openness to trade flows. Further, we agree with the MCC's basic principle of country ownership: local, democratically elected governments should have the strongest voice with respect to where investment funds are placed. Nonetheless, as an agent of the American taxpayer, the MCC also has a fiduciary responsibility to ensure that its funds are used judiciously, supporting economic growth in a way that also advances Washington's democracy agenda.

Beyond the MCC

Going beyond the MCC, we might note that, even with the very best political and economic institutions in place (however defined), and even with the most effective aid programs, incentives to greater investment in, for example, the agricultural sector of developing countries could be greatly undermined if the industrial nations do not open their markets to its exports. In this context we would argue that providing foreign aid to developing nations without granting market access to them is akin to giving a needy student a scholarship to Harvard or Oxford and then denying them employment on graduation because of their race or gender. The disjunction between aid and trade policies is the essence of "policy incoherence."

To be sure, the recognition that young democracies might need this type of international support is hardly new; as early as 1992, Graham T. Allison and Robert Beschel were calling on the advanced industrial states to "nurture the free trading system, resist backsliding... *and... provide open markets for exports from newly established democratic countries...*" (Allison and Beschel 1992, 93, italics added). Again, we must emphasize that continuing tariff and nontariff (e.g., health and safety standards) barriers to trade – especially agriculture trade – and the system of tariff escalation that discourages value-added investment in processed foods significant harm to developing countries (Kapstein 2006).

More generally, the international community would seem to play a major role in the fate of the world's youngest democratizers. As already noted, democracies that emerged in the 1980s and 1990s have had a much better chance of surviving than those that appeared earlier in the postwar era. We suspect that this is because of not only an increase in the "stock" of democracy (the fact that, as countries re-democratize, they increase their amount of democratic culture) but also the structural incentives provided by the international system. More concretely, efforts by the European Union to "lock-in" democracy through the accession process, particularly in Eastern Europe, seem to have played a significant role in promoting consolidation. We will have more to say about the role of the international system in democracy promotion in the following chapter.

With respect to the making of aid policies within the donor countries, we believe that there is a critical need for the assistance community to think more strategically about the ways in which its funding is allocated if one of the key objectives is to support the consolidation of young democratic states (Yang 2006). Specifically, we would argue that policymakers must recognize the sharp differences that exist among young democracies, which make it highly unlikely that a formulaic or "one size fits all" aid package will work. Recognizing these differences and shaping appropriate aid packages will entail a careful and pragmatic balancing act by public officials, and this is a point that is worth emphasizing given the threat of increasing congressional earmarks in the United States and perhaps a growing assertion of ideological values into aid allocations.

In a related vein, the political leaders of young democracies inevitably face intertemporal trade-offs of various kinds, which donors must be sensitive to. For example, foreign aid officials who seek to consolidate young democracies may have to accept that leaders might be forced to make trade-offs between their political (e.g., reelection) and economic (e.g., macroeconomic stabilization) objectives during election years; all "good things" do not necessarily go together, and "win-win" solutions may have to give way to the ranking of priorities (a point emphasized in Carothers 1999). Concretely, the leaders of young democracies seem to be highly tempted to exploit the political business cycle as they pursue their electoral goals, inducing economic volatility. Should foreign aid officials lean on them to stop such behavior, or should they cut these leaders some slack in the hope that what they are doing will lead to democratic consolidation?

At the same time, we would also argue that it is crucial to separate support for individual leaders and support for a nation's institutions: too often in the past it seems as if the two have been confounded. Thus, the United States strongly supported Boris Yeltsin as president of Russia, irrespective of Yeltsin's impact on Russia's nascent institutions. Similarly, the United States has tended to support political leaders who were apparently putting into place "neo-liberal" reforms even at the cost of institutional development. More generally, donors must ask whether political leaders are exploiting the "initial conditions" found in a country to undermine or rollback nascent democratic institutions.

If a hallmark of democracy is the pluralization of economic and political power, then foreign aid policies should be used to bolster that tendency, rather than undermine it, by encouraging the emergence of new classes of economic agents. That is a difficult task because, as already noted, political economy suggests that politicians who wish to control resources, including economic resources, and entrepreneurship could undermine that monopoly. Ironically, aid itself becomes a resource that politicians wish to control and thus there is an element of irony in any effort to decentralize its use. Nonetheless, finding ways to counteract aid's centralizing tendencies should be a major concern of donors of every type, whether bilateral or multilateral, public or private. Although this does not mean that the provision of aid should be blindly decentralized, it does suggest that decentralization could play a useful role as part of a broader aid strategy (Grindle 2007).

In substantive terms, we have argued that the economic and political sides of the aid house must be better coordinated *if* their common objective is democracy promotion and consolidation. Policies that aim to diffuse power on the political side, for example, should be supported by economic programs, such as credit schemes, that provide broad-based opportunities for participation in education and training or human capital formation. Again, a good question for aid officials to ask about their programs and allocations would concern *distributive* effects and whether they help or hinder the pluralization of economic and political power.

How to bring greater coherence and strategic focus to aid delivery in practical or bureaucratic terms is a topic that has been well addressed by others. Lancaster and Van Dusen (2005), for example, suggest a number of possible institutional and organizational fixes that could advance that objective in the United States, including merging the existing aid agencies and giving the U.S. State Department a more prominent role for oversight. In fact, the State Department has already moved in that direction by appointing a foreign aid "czar"; how successful this recent initiative will be remains to be seen (the first czar, Randall Tobias, was forced to resign in 2007 following allegations that he made use of escort services).

In Europe, the situation is no less complex. Each member of the European Union maintains its own aid agencies with their own pet projects (some of which serve in part national, commercial objectives) while they also provide some financial support to EU-wide aid programs, which in some regional cases (namely Eastern Europe) were targeted at helping those countries achieve accession. There appears to be little effort at policy coordination among EU members and recipient governments frequently bemoan the fact that they are overwhelmed by numerous small aid programs. Again, the strategic connection among the various aid initiatives is less than apparent. Perhaps of greatest importance, whereas U.S. policies – for better or for worse – are currently geared toward supporting democratization almost everywhere, European governments tend to be much more reticent about pushing the democracy agenda on recipient countries unlikely to achieve EU accession in the near future (Kopstein 2006). This is to be lamented, as even the *promise* of eventual accession or of closer economic ties to the EU could play a crucial role in "locking-in" democratic institutions in countries where they must now be considered fragile.

To summarize, aid will certainly remain in the foreign policy arsenal for many years to come. Making that aid as effective as possible is therefore a legitimate concern of policy activists and analysts, not to mention of those in recipient nations who require the aid for needed goods, services, and reforms. In this chapter we have argued that aid must support the pluralization of economic and political power in young democracies and that advancing this objective requires a tightly focused program of institutional development on the one hand and economic redistribution (including redistribution of opportunities) on the other. At the same time, we recognize that crafting such a focused program is difficult to achieve given the politicization of aid in both donor and recipient countries, and the many claims that are made on these scarce resources.

But the risk of not developing more effective programs is that democracy promotion assistance will eventually be viewed as a failure; indeed, many influential people have already expressed the view in no uncertain terms that these programs *have failed* (for an insightful review of the debates over democracy promotion, see Rose 2000/2001). Naturally, such a conclusion can undermine political support for assisting young democracies during their early and most fragile years. In this chapter we have tried to show that democracy promotion grants can provide crucial support for countries that are trying to strengthen their nascent institutions and that such support should be a high priority of the international community.

5 Conclusions and Policy Recommendations

There is no easy walk to freedom...
Nelson Mandela, September 21, 1953 (Mandela 2002)

EW CHALLENGES ARE MORE CRUCIAL TO POLICY-MAKERS during this first part of the twenty-first century than ensuring the consolidation and survival of the world's youngest democratic states. The advance of liberal democracy to places yet untouched would mean increasing civil liberties and opportunities for literally millions of people, coupled with much brighter prospects for advancing global commerce and international peace. Conversely, the costs of democratic failure could prove difficult to contain, as authoritarian solutions to political and economic problems gather currency. It is because the stakes are so high that today's foreign assistance programs have made democratization a "core priority" (Carothers 1999), and in fact the public rhetoric in this case has been matched to some extent with increased funding – and even, for better or worse, military action.

To be sure, in only a very few places will foreign assistance and intervention make *the* decisive contribution that determines the fate of a young democracy (and we recall that many scholars consider foreign aid, as a general rule, to be detrimental to political and economic development). If a democracy is to establish and consolidate itself, it will mainly be due to local conditions on the ground coupled with good institutional arrangements and the policy choices made by elected leaders. Still, the fact that democracies have been more likely to consolidate since the 1980s, suggests that the international community is playing a significant role in domestic politics throughout the developing world, for reasons we explore in more detail in a later section of this chapter.

Perhaps the central finding of our work, in line with much contemporary research in political-economy and public policy, is that the institutions that a country builds are critical to its chances for democratic consolidation. We have noted that certain common pathologies seem to arise when societies are deeply divided and when the immediate pressures on leaders to deliver economic benefits to at least some social groups are great. In these cases, as leaders struggle to establish their legitimacy and credibility, an overwhelming temptation exists to grab and centralize power. As Karl Marx put it, "Men make their own history, but they do not make it just as they please; they do not make it under circumstances chosen by themselves, but rather under circumstances found, given and transmitted" (Marx, "The Eighteenth Brumaire of Louis Bonaparte," cited by Rose 2000/2001, 202).

Ironically, this tendency to grab power has sometimes been supported by the international community in the interest of supporting "our man" in power. We assert this is counterproductive and works against the articulation and execution of good public policy. Perhaps of greatest importance to democratic consolidation over the long run may be the degree of effective checks and balances on government leaders, and the redistribution of political and economic power, which requires establishing all manner of formal and informal institutions. When leaders are virtually unconstrained, political and economic performance may be hurt by excessive rent-seeking (but see Glaeser et al. 2004 for a contrary view). In contrast, the checks and balances introduced by electoral and institutional competition can help to motivate "good" behavior. If local leaders and the foreign assistance community draw any conclusion from our study, it is that checks and balances are critical not only to democracy as a political system but to the prospects for sustained economic growth as well.

But what motivates leaders to adopt "good" institutions in the first place? How do they establish the legitimacy and credibility that would engender public trust, enabling them to make long-run decisions that serve the general welfare, and that induce entrepreneurs to invest in the economy? We believe these are among the most significant questions for future research with respect to young democracies, and in the following we provide some more specific suggestions for policy-makers and scholars regarding the advancement of that research agenda.

Lessons for Policy-Makers

What advice does our study provide both to public officials in the foreign assistance community who are striving to help young democracies and to the leaders of those nations who are seeking to consolidate their regimes? We would suggest that our analysis supports the following policy recommendations.

First, do not target economic growth alone in the belief that it will automatically buffer young democracies against the threat of reversal. Rather, by developing political and economic institutions that give all actors a stake in the new system's long-run success, the chances for democratic consolidation will be greatly improved.

Second, echoing remarks made by Allison and Beschel in 1992 (just as democracy promotion was emerging as a priority of U.S. foreign aid and arguably that of the European Union's assistance programs as well), we agree that policy-makers must "realize the inherent limitations in any one-size-fits-all approach to promoting democracy" (Allison and Beschel 1992, 97; see also Rose 2000/2001 for a similar point). As they pointed out then, and as we confirm now in the present study, initial conditions, regional influences, and the quality of political leadership will lead to very different kinds of democratic experience and to wide variations in economic performance. We have seen that these differences may be extremely significant in terms of democratic survival; the stakes of recognizing that fact are thus quite high. This suggests that foreign aid officials must appreciate that young democracies will need assistance packages that are adapted to their special requirements and that ideological preferences and blinders that push one type of policy or program over another will not necessarily serve the cause of democracy very well in the end.

In some cases, this means that the focus of foreign aid should be on helping to develop robust political parties; in others, the emphasis may need to be placed on institutional development and reform or on the promotion of civil society. Carothers (1999) reminds us that the executive branch of government may also need assistance as it establishes its political role and that little aid has been given for this specific purpose. Overall, the type of assistance that we encourage would emphasize the need for checks and balances in young democracies where that institutional framework may be nascent or weak. Clearly, in helping to promote the system of checks and balances, the foreign aid community will likely confront leaders who would prefer a strong and unconstrained executive branch, and many economists have argued that an unconstrained executive is preferable when economic reforms need to be carried out quickly. Our research casts doubt on that "semiauthoritarian" thesis and lends support to those who believe that lasting reforms need broad political legitimacy.

Despite the important differences among young democracies, regional and otherwise, in all cases foreign aid officials must recognize that young democracies are particularly vulnerable during their first five years of existence and that intensive cooperation and support could be required during this time frame and possibly beyond it. Unfortunately, the ability of the world's industrial democracies to devote that kind of sustained attention even to fellow democratic states, fragile as they might be, is questionable at best. Another solution might be to find international "lock-ins" like the European Union, the North American Free Trade Area, or possibly even the World Trade Organization; that is, institutions that will support young democracies over the long haul (a point also made by Rose 2000/2001).

Third, and related, and again echoing comments made years ago by Allison and Beschel (1992), the industrial world must promote trade reforms that favor developing countries and give these states greater voice in the international organizations that now play such a critical role in their economic development (Kapstein 2006). Again, we are not necessarily optimistic about the chances for these policy actions given the political economy of protectionism, but their importance must nonetheless be highlighted, and one can only hope that by repeating this message enough, someone in the industrial world will sit up and listen. Let us make the argument clearly: if the industrial world fails to provide and sustain the background conditions that will help the world's young democracies to thrive, then they will have done much to doom them no matter how much foreign aid they provide. Further, by promoting trade, the industrial world induces new economic agents to enter the marketplace, advancing the cause of democracy as well.

Fourth, the United States in particular must give strong support to its newest foreign aid initiative, the Millennium Challenge Corporation (MCC). The MCC must be allotted the time and policy space to see whether its unique approach to development is yielding benefits in terms of democratic consolidation in the countries with which it has forged its compacts. As we have discussed in Chapter 4, the MCC seems to offer a promising approach to the twin transitions of economic reform and democratic consolidation by focusing on policies – like land tenure reform – that could provide broad-based political support for new regimes, assuming these are supplemented by a host of supporting domestic policies; more on this later.

Fifth, the industrial nations that wish to support democracy in fragile states will need to help provide them with security over several years at least as they develop their institutions and their economies; that is one of the clear lessons that has arisen most dramatically from the ongoing experiences in Afghanistan and Iraq but is hardly limited to the front-page stories. Haiti, East Timor, and many other young democracies could have used prolonged support in the form of a security umbrella as they attempted to make the transition to democracy. Security is not simply required to protect state institutions but also to protect citizens in the act of voting. Further, citizens must be able to make their electoral choices free of any attempts at intimidation. Needless to say, security is also a necessary pre-condition for sustained economic growth.

Sixth, and turning to the leaders of young democracies themselves, it should be recognized that *the evidence suggests that economic reform generally wins popular support so long as its benefits are widely distributed.* This means that as economies liberalize, particular attention needs to be paid to increasing access to new opportunities through the deepening of capital markets and the advancement of educational possibilities – in short, the markets that enable people to improve their life chances. By expanding market access of this kind, leaders will also circumvent potential opponents of reform – like civil servants whose jobs are threatened – and help them make the transition into the economy's growing sectors. In short, redistribution of opportunities if not of income and assets is crucial to democratic consolidation.

Seventh, leaders should be interested to learn that political manipulation of the economy via the political business cycle (PBC) has not proved itself to be a generally successful electoral strategy; to the contrary, voters may "punish" politicians who exploit the cycle and practice fiscal irresponsibility, turning them out of office (Brender and Drazen 2004). To be sure, leaders may feel political pressures during an electoral year to deliver "pork" to various constituent groups, yet they should be aware that this hardly guarantees electoral success. By providing stability, leaders may generate greater political support.

Finally, in those cases where short-term trade-offs appear to exist between political and economic objectives – say where politicians may feel the need to delay privatizations or greater opening to trade – leaders must nonetheless provide a timetable by which these policies will be enacted to give confidence to investors that policy is moving in a growth-enhancing direction. To be sure, each country will formulate its own timetable, and it is important that the international community avoids placing excessive pressure on the leaders of young democracies because of ideological preferences for free trade or foreign direct investment. Developing world governments may rightly feel that they need some policy space or room to maneuver as they consolidate their democracies, and surely something like a five-year time horizon seems more than reasonable as they experiment with meeting the demands of the dual transition to democracy and more open markets.

Directions for Future Research

Although recent years have witnessed a dramatic increase in the number of studies concerned with young democracies in the developing world, clearly more much research needs to be done to help us address some fundamental theoretical puzzles and policy-relevant problems. As already noted, we need to learn more about how "good" incentives can be created for leaders to invest in institutions and policies that are likely to be supportive of democracy-building and that help to diffuse political and economic power. Additionally, we need to know more about the actors who are responsible for democratic reversals. Do these actors come predominantly from within or outside the democratic regime? Do they represent particular groups (e.g. the military) or are they mass movements?

Both cross-country and case study research will be valuable in answering these sorts of questions, and we hope that more scholars will adopt "multimethodological" approaches to their research. To take a prominent contemporary example that deserves more scholarly research, consider the path of democratization in Indonesia. Whereas only a few years ago many observers doubted the ability of post-Suharto Indonesia to build a set of durable democratic institutions, it appears that the leadership has worked hard in that direction. Even if it is too soon to tell whether its efforts will succeed, there is undoubtedly much that scholars and policy-makers can learn from the choices that leaders have made there and why they made them. Why has domestic politics (to date at least) supported the democratic experiment? What role has the international community played? A study of Indonesia, alongside other significant cases, could potentially reveal much about the issues we have covered in this book.

Elections, Parties, and Economic Performance

As is clear from the number of citations, our research has been powerfully influenced by the work of Samuel P. Huntington (1991) and Philip Keefer (2007a, 2007b). In particular, these authors have stressed the primordial importance of credibility and legitimacy if young democracies are to consolidate. But how do leaders achieve credibility and legitimacy with the voting public? The answer is that we really do not know; surely, there can be few research questions of greater importance.

To explore it in greater depth, one might look at the PBC as a proxy of the problem at hand. Intriguingly, scholars have demonstrated that manipulation of the PBC seems to decrease with the age and/or wealth of the democracy; again, the relationship between politics and economics changes over time. Further, research has shown that the PBC is much less important overall in the advanced industrial countries than it is in many developing countries, whereas across developing countries its amplitude varies greatly (at least until recently, where convergence seems to be taking place with respect to macroeconomic policy). How do we explain these effects? An answer to that question would bring us closer to understanding issues of credibility and legitimacy and of how politicians interact with the voting public.

And this suggests the need for deeper analyses of the electoral process in the developing world and its impact on economic performance. Are the economic problems of developing countries so great that elected leaders have little choice but to respond with immediate fixes, no matter the long-run political and economic consequences? Or are the leaders so weak politically that they feel they must deliver the goods today if they are to stay in office tomorrow? Paying close attention to elections and to the role of candidates and political parties should be a high priority of scholars who focus on young democratic states (Carbone 2003; Kaplan 2006).

We also see a need for more research into the medium- and long-term effects of the PBC on economic performance and democratic governance. Do the negative repercussions of the volatility introduced by the PBC wane over time or do they remain significant? More generally, how do governments today overcome the hangover produced by the spending binges or raids on the public purse that were carried out yesterday? Surprisingly little academic research has investigated the effects of the PBC on long-run growth and policy-making over time, but that would seem a key issue for those who believe that poor economic performance undermines young democratic regimes.

Much of the work on the relationship between electoral democracy and economic policy is driven by the assumption of a "median" or "decisive" voter, and that assumption has carried over to the literature on the developing world. Acemoglu and Robinson (2006), for example, model the demand for democracy as being fundamentally driven by the median voter and her interest in redistributive economic policies. Yet we have seen little empirical discussion of who the median voter actually is in the world's young democracies and how, in fact, she has fared in practice under the new regime. We also have very little evidence on redistribution in the world's youngest democracies, a gap that must be filled if we are to understand the political economy of these states and their prospects for consolidation.

The evidence we have accumulated to date poses some real puzzles for the median voter thesis. Kapstein and Milanovic (2003), for example, have shown that greater openness has not been good for median voters in most of the developing world, at least in terms of their relative incomes. To the contrary, in poor developing countries that have opened their markets, income inequality has risen more than in those that remained relatively closed. They also do not even find any evidence that income transfers or social safety nets are targeted at the median voter. There are good reasons for why that might be the case in practice (e.g., the inability of median voters to organize or "collective action" problems) but again a great deal of work is needed on this supposedly crucial actor in the electoral process.

We have argued throughout this book that programmatic political parties are of great importance to both democratic consolidation and economic performance. Yet research on the evolution of these parties in young democratizers has lagged (though, for important exceptions, see Carothers 2004, 2006; on Africa in particular see Carbone 2003). How do parties become established in the first place? What are their programs are and which voters do they attract? What should the international community do to encourage such parties? And should limits be placed on what parties participate in political life? All these are questions of first-order importance for the "democracy and development" agenda.

The question of elections and parties also causes us to consider the role of elites in the process of democratic consolidation. Although elite unification may or may not be the "vital step" in determining whether a democracy will ultimately consolidate (Higley and Burton 1989), a number of cases (e.g., Thailand and Pakistan) suggest that the importance of elite cohesion is considerable. How do elites interact with parties and the electoral process in advancing their interests? What sorts of coalitions do they seek to build? Understanding different elite groups and how their interests can be reconciled via the electoral process remains a powerful and important challenge for research into the correlates of democratic consolidation.

Institutions, Ideas, and Democracy

In this monograph we have reported on a number of studies that relate a democracy's economic performance and chances of consolidation to its institutional configuration (e.g., parliamentary vs presidential), and have added to that work by observing that institutional checks and balances serve an important stabilizing function no matter what the constitutional arrangement; of course, the presence of that mechanism constitutes a primary difference between them and authoritarian states. Yet we know little about *why* or under what conditions political leaders would choose a regime type characterized by checks and balances over one with a strong presidency. Is that choice due to the initial conditions that young democracies face or the circumstances under which governments came to power (Cheibub 2006, for example, emphasizes the legacy effects of military regimes), or do other factors (e.g., regional and international influences) come into play?

Democracy promotion funds, for example, have been used to bring constitutional experts to countries to help them write their foundational documents. Is this sort of advice influential in shaping outcomes? Understanding more about how institutions are chosen and designed in the world's young democracies would be an extremely useful contribution to the political economy literature.

Academic research also points to the critical role of such "extrapolitical" institutions as independent central banks and judiciaries in providing the background conditions that promote policy credibility and in turn motivate savings and investment. Again, under what circumstances are such institutions supported and maintained by political and economic elites? Independent central banks, for example, are a relatively recent phenomenon, but since the mid-1950s they have spread globally. As with the case of constitution-writing and institutional design, this suggests that there may be international forces at work in their diffusion: what are those forces and how have they influenced local political environments (Elkins and Simmons 2004)?

These questions, in turn, lead us to contemplate the role of *ideas* more generally in the making of public policy and institutional configurations in the world's young democracies – something we have not focused on in this monograph. We would assert, however, that the ideas that policy-makers have about how the world works play a significant role in their decision-making. Tracing these ideas and analyzing how they shape public policy and institutional design continues to present a major challenge to researchers.

Any discussion of the role of institutions and ideas must eventually confront the fundamental theoretical problem – but one that is crucial to policy-makers as well – of institutional *change*, particularly of how it occurs and for what reasons. In much of the political economy literature, institutions are conceived of as equilibrium sets of rules and norms around which actors' behavioral expectations converge. Yet in this game-theoretic approach, it is not obvious how one understands the process of institutional change other than via an exogenous shock.

Institutions, however, may change endogenously, and understanding how that can occur is absolutely essential to policy-relevant scholarship (Greif and Laitin 2004; Acemoglu and Robinson 2006). To put this bluntly, without theories of reform and change it is very difficult to provide compelling advice to public officials. There is no shortage of ideas for improving the economic policies and performance of nations – introduce the rule of law, eliminate corruption, stabilize the economy, and so forth – but how to put these ideas into effect is the crucial issue, and that requires some notion of politically feasible or welfare-enhancing change (Kapstein 2006). Fortunately, the problem of institutional change is now becoming a central issue for political economists.

The International Political Economy of Democratic Survival

As we have seen, democracies that have emerged since the 1970s have had a much better shot at survival than those born earlier in the twentieth century. This fact, when combined with the global "third wave" of democratization that began in Western Europe in the early 1970s and since has spread around the world, naturally makes us think about the international sources of democratization and how international forces may influence the political economy of young democratic states and their prospects for survival. This is an area in which much more work needs to be done, but several suggestive theories have been offered. We sketch them here in the hope they encourage others to pursue this trail.

First, Acemoglu and Robinson (2006) have posited that globalization can promote democratization by facilitating capital flight. The logic stems from their model of the democratization process, which is based on a game between rich and poor. The rich are willing to redistribute a little (but not a lot) in return for strong property rights and of course they give the poor the franchise. With globalization, the poor's ability to expropriate is limited, so the rich have greater faith in democracy's staying power. Unfortunately, this only works if the rich have most of their assets in financial instruments. If wealth is concentrated in land, then capital flight would seemingly do little to enhance their security.

A *second* pathway focuses on the relationship between globalization and democratic ideas. As Eichengreen and Leblang (2006) argue, "the exchange of goods and services is a conduit for the exchange of ideas, and a more diverse stock of ideas encourages political competition." Further, they assert that "in financially open economies, the government and central bank must be transparent in order to retain the confidence of the markets, and transparency spells doom for autocratic regimes." Again, Eichengreen and Leblang seemingly downplay the ability of autocratic regimes to shape globalization in a way that strengthens rather than undermines them, with cases in point provided by Middle East oil suppliers and China, at least to the present era. After all, the turn to globalization is not the same thing as turning the light switch to "on," which is merely a binary choice; there are many mixes between openness and closure that governments can choose.

Third, scholars have long posited that a given regime type might have "contagion effects" within a certain region (for a recent example see Persson and Tabellini 2006). If most states in, say, Africa or Latin America become democratic, it is more likely that the remaining states will become democratic as well.

Fourth, powerful democratic anchors like the European Union or other international bodies, when willing to expand to new member states, can have a powerful influence on a given region's prospects for democratization (see Pevehouse 2002). But how strong is that effect in fact?

Larrabbee (2006), for example, has recently raised concerns over the potential for democratic backsliding in Eastern Europe. We have also noted the political pressure that Russia has placed on some of its neighbors, perhaps offsetting democratic tendencies. Thus, how "locks" are established and how they might be broken is a topic of central significance for understanding the international politics of democratization.

Finally, the spread of democracy might reflect the regime type of the international system's most powerful nation, namely the United States, at least since the collapse of the Soviet Union. America's rhetorical preference for democracy might cause rulers elsewhere to recognize that they are more likely to receive the things they want from Washington, such as foreign aid, military support, open markets, and entry to international organizations, if they adopt America's democratic form as well. If this is the case, China's growing role in trade with and aid to countries in Africa and Latin America may have negative repercussions for the survival of democracy.

In short, research posits a number of pathways by which the international system can "press down" on domestic societies and cause them to make the transition from authoritarianism to democracy. Each of these routes, however, is in need of much more theoretical elaboration and empirical testing. A rich research agenda awaits those who venture into this particular terrain (Pevehouse 2002; Mansfield and Pevehouse 2006).

Concluding Thoughts

Writing many years ago, Higley and Burton (1989) stated that "Stable democracies do not emerge simply by writing constitutions, holding elections, expanding human rights, accelerating economic growth, or exterminating leftist insurgencies. The vital step is the consensual unification of previously disunited elites." Whether or not one agrees with their ultimate conclusion, they correctly point to the complexity of the democratic experience. If democracy ultimately consolidates in a given country, it is because its leaders will have somehow convinced the polity that this regime type does a better job of reconciling the diverse needs of divided societies than does the authoritarian alternative.

In this study we have provided reasons for both hope and caution as we observe the evolution of today's newly established democratic regimes. On the one hand, we now know that democracy is compatible with economic reform and sustained development, an idea that not so long ago was considered dubious by many social scientists, if not policy-makers, who believed that the strong rule of a "man on horseback" was needed to suppress consumption in favor of investment. On the other, we also know that democratizers tend to be fragile during their early years of existence, *particularly when those regimes lack an elaborate system of checks and balances to constrain executive power.*

At the same time, we have further seen that the democracies that have emerged in recent decades have had a better shot at consolidation than those that appeared on the world scene in earlier postwar decades. The international community thus undoubtedly has a positive role to play in helping these regimes build solid institutional foundations that create public confidence in the democratic future. In that light, signs that the "third wave" of democracy may now be retreating are troubling, making an analysis of what ails the world's young democracies all the more pertinent.

Overall, our findings show that the *type* of democratic institutions that are built, and the *type* of economic growth that is generated, may matter greatly to the process of democratic consolidation; after all, one of democracy's greatest promises is the diffusion of wealth and power. To be sure, "initial conditions" may influence a government's chances for survival by creating particular incentives for leaders, but we should not underestimate the importance of political agency. We can only hope that our work has revealed some of the ways in which careful institu-tional design, bolstered by the international community, can serve the cause of consolidation in the world's youngest democratic states.

Appendix 1 Methodology

Definition of Democracy

Classifying governments as democratic or nondemocratic, as well as identifying episodes of political change as democratizations, is fraught with theoretical and practical pitfalls. For example, Milanovic (2005) finds that when using the Polity IV index of democracy, which has a 20-point scale (-10 to $+10$) that ranks regimes from most authoritarian to most democratic, where the analyst draws the line (e.g., at 0 or at $+1$) between democracy and authoritarianism has a significant impact on the findings. Our analysis attempts to avoid engaging with this particular issue by first identifying democratizations and then classifying the regime prior to the democratization as undemocratic and the resulting regime as a new democracy. Consequently, a more accurate term for the countries that we analyze might be "newly democratized" countries rather than democracies.

In building our democratization data set, we have relied on the Polity IV data set on political regime characteristics and transitions (Marshall and Jaggers 2005). Although the aggregation of the various components of the Polity score has been characterized as problematic (Munck and Verkuilen 2002), the extensive disaggregated data on regime characteristics that the Polity project makes available led us to use this measure. In particular, we employ the Polity IV score for the level of constraints on the executive, a factor not assessed by, for example, the classification developed by Przeworski et al. (2000). Consequently, we found the Polity data the most appropriate for our purposes.

We define "democratizations" based on the "Major Democratic Transitions" in the Polity data set (Marshall and Jaggers 2005). Such transitions involve a 6-point or greater increase (e.g., from −3 to +3) in the overall Polity score over a period of three or fewer years, and we note this definition is also used by Rodrik and Wacziarg (2005) and Rigobon and Rodrik (2004), among others. Whereas the Polity data take pains to identify and flag transition periods between regimes, our analysis considers democratizations to have taken place only when the transitions have actually "finished" and led to a democratic regime. For example, Polity views Mexico as undergoing a gradual democratic transition from 1994 to 1997, with each of those four years considered to have contained a "Major Democratic Transition." Our analysis classifies 1997 as the first year of the new democracy, because it was in that year the new, more democratic system was, at least according to Polity, fully in place. We classify countries as undergoing reversals, that is, ceasing to be democracies, when they experience what the Polity data set terms an "adverse regime transition," an antidemocratic "revolutionary transformation in the mode of governance" (Marshall and Jaggers 2005, 35).

We freely confess that, in theory, our methodology is problematic for at least two reasons, which fortunately do not arise in practice with the data. First, our approach allows for the possibility of two successive democratizations with no intervening reversal or transition, which is theoretically problematic because the academic literature on democratization generally conceptualizes it as an "event," with subsequent increases in the quality of democracy characterized as steps toward consolidation. However, this does not actually occur in the Polity data after 1960. In two cases − Guatemala in the 1970s and Thailand in 1991 − Polity data identify one or more "negative regime changes" (as opposed to a more serious "adverse regime transition") between episodes of democratization. In these situations, the first of these setbacks to democracy was coded as a democratic reversal in our data set.

A second and related issue stems from focusing on quantitative changes rather than qualitative levels to separate democracies from non-democracies. In theory, a 6-point "Major Democratic Transition" could bring a country from a higher to a lower authoritarian score (e.g., −10 to −4), resulting in an undemocratic government being mistakenly classified as having become democratic. Again, this does not in fact occur in the data set, and all regime changes classified as democratizations in this study produced a positive Polity score. Four have a score of 1 (Pakistan 1962, Sierra Leone 1968, Cambodia 1993, Ethiopia 1995), eight have a score of 2, seven with a score of 3, nine with a score of 4, and twelve with a score of 5.

In defining democracy, a methodological issue arises regarding the treatment of newly independent states. Some of the most widely cited empirical studies of the effects of democracy on economic policy and performance did not incorporate data from the newly independent nations of the former Soviet bloc, leading scholars to question the robustness of the findings. For those studies produced since 1990, this is partly because no convention exists among scholars regarding the political regime classification of these states. Presumably, one could investigate the system of government that prevailed in each newly independent country prior to independence and then judge whether independence marked a transition to democracy or the consolidation of already extant democratic institutions. In this case, many of the former Soviet republics would be classified as new democracies because the USSR was clearly not a democracy. The situation would be less clear in the case of, for example, British colonies that had some sort of representative assembly, albeit with limited decision-making power, prior to independence. For the sake of completeness and consistency, not to mention simplicity, our study classifies all newly independent countries with positive Polity scores as new democracies. This results in the inclusion of 32 additional new democracies, including 17 countries that were previously part of the Soviet Union, Yugoslavia, or Czechoslovakia. Our data set does not include the former Soviet republics Turkmenistan, Tajikistan, Kyrgyzstan, Uzbekistan, and Kazakhstan, which have never attained a positive Polity score.

TABLE A1.1. *Democratizations by region and decade*

	1960s	1970s	1980s	1990s	After 2000	Total
Total	26	20	17	51	9	123
Latin America	6	3	11	5	1	26
Western Europe	1	3	0	0	0	4
Eastern Europe	0	0	0	19	2	21
Sub-Saharan Africa	15	6	2	18	5	46
Middle East-N. Africa	0	1	1	1	0	3
Asia	4	7	3	8	1	23

Source: Polity IV, author's calculations.

Democratization Data Set

The methodology described earlier identifies 123 episodes of democratization during the period from 1960 to 2004 (a list of these is included in Appendix 2). Of these democratizations, 26 took place in Latin America, 4 were in Western Europe, 21 in Eastern Europe, 46 in sub-Saharan Africa, 3 in the Middle East and North Africa region, and 23 in Asia. Table A1.1 makes clear the importance of regional trends in the timing of democratizations, with sub-Saharan African countries – mainly those gaining independence – making up the majority of democratizations in the 1960s and 1970s. By contrast, 11 of 17 democratizations in the 1980s took place in Latin America, whereas over 70 percent of

TABLE A1.2. *Democratizations by region and outcome*

	Sustained	Reversed
Total	67	56
Latin America	17	9
Western Europe	3	1
Eastern Europe	19	2
Sub-Saharan Africa	17	29
Middle East-N. Africa	1	2
Asia	10	13

Source: Polity IV, author's calculations.

democratizations in the 1990s occurred in Eastern Europe and sub-Saharan Africa.

Of the regimes created by these democratizations, 67 survived through 2004, the end of our sample period, whereas 56 had been reversed. Although sub-Saharan Africa has been the site of nearly twice as many democratizations as any other region, less than half of these have been sustained, with 63 percent of African democratizations ending in reversal (see Table A1.2). Latin American and Asian democratizers have also exhibited limited durability, with nearly 35 percent and 57 percent, respectively, undergoing reversal. By contrast, over 90 percent of Eastern European democratizations had been sustained as of 2004. North Africa and the Middle East have seen few democratizations, sustained or otherwise. In the post-1960 period, Turkey had one democratization that was reversed and another that was sustained. Reforms in Iran in the late 1990s resulted in it being qualified as a democratizer in 1997, but a rollback of these reforms in 2003 meant that this democratization was classified as having been reversed.[1]

---

[1] Between 1997 and 2003, Polity assigned Iran a score of three, a ranking also applied to South Korea in the late 1960s and Malaysia since 1995. In 2004, Iran's Polity score fell to −6.

Appendix 2 List of Young Democracies

TABLE A2.1. *Young democracies in Latin America*

Country	Year of democratization	Year of reversal (if any)
Dominican Republic	1962	1963
Trinidad	1962	
Dominican Republic	1978	
Haiti	1990	1991
Haiti	1994	1999
Guatemala	1966	1970
Honduras	1982	
El Salvador	1984	
Guatemala	1986	
Panama	1989	
Nicaragua	1990	
Mexico	1997	
Peru	1963	1968
Guyana	1966	1978
Ecuador	1968	1970
Argentina	1973	1976
Ecuador	1979	
Peru	1980	1992
Bolivia	1982	
Argentina	1983	
Brazil	1985	
Uruguay	1985	
Paraguay	1989	
Chile	1989	
Guyana	1992	
Peru	2001	

TABLE A2.2. *Young democracies in Western Europe*

Country	Year of democratization	Year of reversal (if any)
Cyprus	1960	1963
Greece	1975	
Portugal	1976	
Spain	1978	

TABLE A2.3. *Young democracies in Eastern Europe*

Country	Year of democratization	Year of reversal (if any)
Hungary	1990	
Czech Republic	1990	
Bulgaria	1990	
Romania	1990	
Poland	1991	
Albania	1992	
Macedonia	1991	
Slovenia	1991	
Moldova	1991	
Croatia	2000	
Yugoslavia	2000	
Estonia	1991	
Latvia	1991	
Lithuania	1991	
Ukraine	1991	
Belarus	1991	1995
Armenia	1991	1995
Georgia	1991	
Russia	1992	
Slovakia	1993	
Armenia	1998	

TABLE A2.4. *Young democracies in sub-Saharan Africa*

Country	Year of democratization	Year of reversal (if any)
Benin	1960	1963
Nigeria	1960	1964
Sierra Leone	1961	1967
Gambia	1965	1994
Equatorial Guinea	1968	1969
Sierra Leone	1968	1971
Ghana	1970	1972
Burkina Faso	1978	1980
Ghana	1979	1981
Nigeria	1979	1984
Benin	1991	
Mali	1992	
Niger	1992	1996
Ghana	1992	
Guinea-Bissau	1994	1998
Sierra Leone	1996	1997
Niger	1999	
Nigeria	1999	
Senegal	2000	
Ivory Coast	2000	2002
Congo Brazzaville	1960	1963
Congo Brazzaville	1992	1997
Central African Republic	1993	2003
Somalia	1960	1969
Uganda	1962	1966
Kenya	1963	1969
Sudan	1965	1969
Mozambique	1994	
Ethiopia	1995	
Djibouti	1999	
Kenya	2002	
Zambia	1964	1972
Lesotho	1966	1970
Botswana	1966	
Zimbabwe	1970	1987
Namibia	1990	
Zambia	1991	
Lesotho	1993	1998
Malawi	1994	
Mauritius	1968	
Comoros	1975	1976
Comoros	1990	1995
Madagascar	1992	
Comoros	2004	

TABLE A2.5. *Young democracies in the Middle East-North Africa*

Country	Year of democratization	Year of reversal (if any)
Turkey	1973	1980
Turkey	1983	
Iran	1997	2004

TABLE A2.6. *Young democracies in Asia*

Country	Year of democratization	Year of reversal (if any)
South Korea	1960	1961
South Korea	1963	1972
South Korea	1988	
Mongolia	1992	
Taiwan	1992	
Pakistan	1962	1971
Bangladesh	1972	1974
Pakistan	1973	1977
Pakistan	1988	1999
Nepal	1990	2002
Bangladesh	1991	
Thailand	1969	1971
Thailand	1974	1976
Thailand	1978	1991
Thailand	1992	
Cambodia	1993	1997
Fiji	1970	1987
Papua New Guinea	1975	
Solomon Islands	1978	2000
Philippines	1987	
Fiji	1990	
Indonesia	1999	
East Timor	2002	

References

Acemoglu, Daron, Simon Johnson, and James A. Robinson. 2005. Institutions as the Fundamental Cause of Long-Run Growth. *Handbook of Economic Growth*. Eds. Philippe Aghion and Stephen Durlauf. Amsterdam: North Holland.

Acemoglu, Daron, and James Robinson. 2006. *Economic Origins of Democracy and Dictatorship*. New York: Cambridge University Press.

Adsera, Alicia, and Carles Boix. 2004. Constitutional Engineering and the Stability of Democracies. Paper presented to the Annual Conference of the International Society for New Institutional Economics. Tucson, Arizona, September 30–October 3, 2004.

Aizenman, Joshua, and Nancy Marion. 1999. Volatility and Investment: Interpreting Evidence from Developing Countries. *Economica* 66: 157–79.

Alesina, Alberto, Arnaud Devleeschauwer, William Easterly, Sergio Kurlat, and Romain Wacziarg. 2003. Fractionalization. *Journal of Economic Growth* 8: 155–94.

Alesina, Alberto, and Nouriel Roubini with Gerald Cohen. 1997. *Political Cycles and the Macroeconomy*. Cambridge, MA: MIT Press.

Allcott, Hunt, Daniel Lederman, and Ramón López. 2006. Political Institutions, Inequality, and Agricultural Growth: The Public Expenditure Connection. World Bank Policy Research Working Paper 3902. Washington, DC: World Bank.

Allison, Graham T., and Robert Beschel. 1992. Can the United States Promote Democracy? *Political Science Quarterly* 107(1): 81–98.

Bardhan, Pranab, and Tsung-Tao Yang. 2004. Political Competition in Economic Perspective. BREAD Working Paper 78. Cambridge, MA: Harvard University.

Beck, Thorsten, and Luc Laeven. 2005. Institution Building and Growth in Transition Economies. World Bank Policy Research Working Paper 3657. Washington, DC: World Bank.

Bernhard, Michael, Christopher Reenock, and Timothy Nordstrom. 2001. Economic Performance, Institutional Intermediation, and Democratic Survival. *Journal of Politics* 63(3): 775–803.

Bernhard, Michael, Christopher Reenock, and Timothy Nordstrom. 2003. Economic Performance and Democratic Survival in New Democracies: Is There a Honeymoon? *Comparative Political Studies* 36(4): 404–31.

Bertrand, Jacques. 1998. Growth and Democracy in Southeast Asia. *Comparative Politics* 30(3): 355–75.

Bienen, Henry, and Jeffrey Herbst. 1996. The Relationship between Political and Economic Reform in Africa. *Comparative Politics* 29(2):23–42.

Block, Steven A. 2002. Elections, Electoral Competitiveness, and Political Budget Cycles in Developing Countries. Harvard University Center for International Development Working Paper 78. Cambridge, MA: Harvard University.

Block, Steven, A. 2005. Counting the Investor Vote: Political Business Cycle Effects on Sovereign Bond Spreads in Developing Countries. *Journal of International Business Studies* 36(1): 62–88.

Block, Steven A., Karen E. Ferree, and Smita Singh. 2003. Multiparty Competition, Founding Elections, and Political Business Cycles in Africa. *Journal of African Economies* 12(3): 444–68.

Box-Steffensmeier, Janet M and, Bradford S. Jones. 2004. *Event History Modelling: A Guide for Social Scientists.* Cambridge: Cambridge University Press.

Brender, Adi, and Allan Drazen. 2004. Political Budget Cycles in New Versus Established Economies. NBER Working Paper 10539. Cambridge, MA: National Bureau of Economic Research.

Bresser Pereira, Luis Carlos, José Maria Maravall, and Adam Przeworski. 1993. *Economic Reforms in New Democracies: A Social Democratic Approach.* Cambridge: Cambridge University Press.

Bruce, John. 1996. *Country Profiles of Land Tenure, Africa.* Madison, WI: Land Tenure Center, University of Wisconsin.

Bueno de Mesquita, Bruce, Alastair Smith, Randolph M. Siverson, and James D. Morrow. 2003. *The Logic of Political Survival.* Cambridge, MA: MIT Press.

Bunce, Valerie. 2001. Democratization and Economic Reform. *Annual Review of Political Science* 4: 43–65.

Byman, Daniel L., and Kenneth M. Pollack. 2003. Democracy in Iraq? *The Washington Quarterly* 26(3): 119–36.

Carbone, Giovanni M. 2003. Developing Multi-Party Politics: Stability and Change in Ghana and Mozambique. Crisis States Research Centre Working Papers No. 36 (November). London: London School of Economics.

Carothers, Thomas. 1999. *Aiding Democracy Abroad*. Washington, DC: Carnegie Endowment for International Peace.

Carothers, Thomas. 2004. *Political Party Aid: Issues for Reflection and Discussion*. Unpublished Memorandum for the Swedish International Development Agency.

Carothers, Thomas. 2006. *Confronting the Weakest Link: Aiding Political Parties in New Democracies*. Washington, DC: Carnegie Endowment for International Peace.

Carothers, Thomas. 2007. A Quarter Century of Promoting Democracy. *Journal of Democracy* 18(1): 112–18.

Case, William F. 2001. Thai Democracy, 2001: Out of Equilibrium. *Asian Survey* 41(3): 525–47.

Centeno, Miguel Angel. 1994. Between Rocky Democracies and Hard Markets: Dilemmas of the Double Transition. *Annual Review of Sociology* 20: 125–47.

Cheibub, Jose Antonio. 2006. Presidentialism, Electoral Identifiability, and Budget Balances in Democratic Systems. *American Political Science Review* 100(3): 353–68.

Clemens, Michael, Charles Kenny, and Todd Moss. 2004. The Trouble with the MDGs: Confronting Expectations of Aid and Development Success. Center for Global Development Working Paper 40. Washington, DC: Center for Global Development.

Collins, Wilkie. (1868/1998). *The Moonstone*. London: Penguin Classics.

De Soto, Hernando. 2003. *The Mystery of Capital*. New York: Basic Books.

Dethier, Jean-Jacques, Hafez Ghanem, and Edda Zoli. 1999. Does Democracy Facilitate the Economic Transition? World Bank Policy Research Working Paper 2194. Washington, DC: World Bank.

Diamond, Jared. 2001. *Guns, Germs and Steel*. New York: W. W. Norton.

Diamond, Larry. 1999. *Developing Democracy: Toward Consolidation*. Baltimore, MD: Johns Hopkins University Press.

Diamond, Larry. 2005. Democracy, Development and Good Governance: The Inseparable Links. *Annual Democracy and Governance Lecture.* Accra, Ghana: Center for Democratic Development.

Downs, Anthony. 1957. *An Economic Theory of Democracy.* New York: Harpers.

Dornbusch, Rudiger, and Sebastian Edwards. 1991. The Macroeconomics of Populism. *The Macroeconomics of Populism in Latin America.* Eds. Rudiger Dornbusch and Sebastian Edwards. Chicago: University of Chicago Press.

Drazen, Allan. 2001. *The Political Economy of Macroeconomics.* Princeton, NJ: Princeton University Press.

Easterly, William, and Ross Levine. 1997. Africa's Growth Tragedy: Policies and Ethnic Divisions. *Quarterly Journal of Economics* 111(4): 1203–50.

Economic Commission on Latin America and the Caribbean. 2006. *Preliminary Overview of the Economies of Latin America and the Caribbean.* Santiago: Economic Commission on Latin America and the Caribbean.

Eichengreen, Barry, and David Leblang. 2006. Democracy and Globalization. NBER Working Paper 12450. Cambridge, MA: National Bureau of Economic Research.

Elkins, Zachary, and Beth Simmons. 2004. The Globalization of Liberalization: Policy Diffusion in the International Political Economy. *American Political Science Review* 98(1): 171–89.

Elster, Jon. 1989. *The Cement of Society: A Survey of Social Order.* Cambridge University Press.

Epstein, David L., Robert Bates, Jack Goldstone, Ida Kristensen, and Sharyn O'Halloran. 2006. Democratic Transitions. *American Journal of Political Science* 50(3): 551–69.

Fidrmuc, Jan. 2001. Democracy in Transition Economies: Grease or Sand in the Wheels of Growth? EIB Papers 6: 24–40.

Field, Erica and Maximo Torero. 2006. Do Property Titles Increase Credit Access Among the Urban Poor? Evidence from a Nationwide Titling Program. Mimeo, Harvard University.

Finkel, Steven, Anabel Perez-Linan, and Mitchell Seligson. 2006. *Effects of US Foreign Assistance on Democracy Building: Final Report.* Washington, DC: U.S. Agency for International Development.

Fish, M. Steven. 2001. The Dynamics of Democratic Erosion. *Postcommunism and the Theory of Democracy.* Eds. Richard D. Anderson, M. Steven

Fish, Stephen E. Hanson, and Philip G. Roeder. Princeton, NJ: Princeton University Press.

Frank, Thomas. 2004. *What's the Matter with Kansas?* New York: Henry Holt.

Galiani, Sebastian, and Ernesto Schargrodsky. 2006. Property Rights for the Poor: Effects of Land Titling. Universidad Torcuato di Tella Business School Working Paper 06/2005. Buenos Aires: Universidad Torcuato di Tella.

Gasiorowski, Mark J., and Timothy J. Power. 1998. Institutional Design and Democratic Consolidation in the Third World. *Comparative Political Studies* 30(2): 123–55.

Gerring, John, Philip Bond, William T. Barndt, and Carola Moreno. 2005. Democracy and Economic Growth: A Historical Perspective. *World Politics* 57: 323–64.

Glaeser, Edward, Raphael La Porta, Florencio Lopez-de-Silanes, and Andrei Shleifer. 2004. Do Institutions Cause Growth? *Journal of Economic Growth* 9: 271–304.

Goldstein, Markus, and Christopher Udry. 2005. The Profits of Power: Land Rights and Agricultural Investment in Ghana. Yale University Economic Growth Center Working Paper 929. New Haven, CT: Yale University.

Gradstein, Mark. 2005. Democracy, Property Rights, Redistribution and Economic Growth. Center for Economic Policy Research Working Paper DP5130. London: Center for Economic Policy Research.

Greif, Avner, and David Laitin. 2004. A Theory of Endogenous Institutional Change. *American Political Science Review* 98(4): 633–52.

Grindle, Merilee S. 2007. *Going Local: Decentralization, Democratization, and the Promise of Good Governance.* Princeton, NJ: Princeton University Press.

Guillaume, Dominique, and David Stasavage. 1999. Making and Breaking Monetary Policy Rules: The Experience of African Countries. Centre for the Study of African Economies Working Paper 99-2. Oxford: Oxford University.

Haggard, Stephan, and Robert Kaufman. 1995. *The Political Economy of Democratic Transitions.* Princeton, NJ: Princeton University Press.

Hellman, Joel. 1998. Winner Takes All: The Politics of Partial Reform in Postcommunist Transition. *World Politics* 50: 203–34.

Higley, John, and Michael G. Burton. 1989. The Elite Variable in Democratic Transitions and Breakdowns. *American Sociological Review* 54(1): 17–32.

Huntington, Samuel P. 1968. *Political Order in Changing Societies*. New Haven, CT: Yale University Press.

Huntington, Samuel P. 1991. *The Third Wave: Democratization in the Late Twentieth Century*. Norman: University of Oklahoma Press.

Jackman, Robert W. 1986. Elections and the Democratic Class Struggle. *World Politics* 39(1): 123–46.

Kaplan, Stephen. 2006. Do Elections Hurt Developing Economies? Unpublished Manuscript.

Kapstein, Ethan B. 2004. Behavioral Foundations of Democracy and Development. Center for Global Development Working Paper 52. Washington, DC: Center for Global Development.

Kapstein, Ethan B. 2006. *Economic Justice in an Unfair World: Toward a Level Playing Field*. Princeton, NJ: Princeton University Press.

Kapstein, Ethan B., and Branko Milanovic. 2003. *Income and Influence: Social Policy in Emerging Market Economies*. Kalamazoo, MI: Upjohn Institute.

Keefer, Philip. 2004. A Review of the Political Economy of Governance. 2004. World Bank Policy Research Working Paper 3315. Washington, DC: World Bank.

Keefer, Philip. 2005. Democratization and Clientelism: Why Are Young Democracies Badly Governed? World Bank Policy Research Working Paper 3594. Washington, DC: World Bank.

Keefer, Philip. 2007a. The Political Economy of Development. *The Oxford Handbook of Comparative Politics*. Eds. Carles Boix and Susan C. Stokes. New York: Oxford University Press.

Keefer, Philip. 2007b. Clientelism, Credibility and the Policy Choices of Young Democracies. *American Journal of Political Science* 51(4): 804–21.

Keefer, Philip, and Stuti Khemani. 2005. Democracy, Public Expenditures, and the Poor: Understanding Political Incentives for Providing Public Services. *The World Bank Research Observer* 20(1): 1–27

Keefer, Philip, and David Stasavage. 2003. The Limits of Delegation: Veto Players, Central Bank Independence, and the Credibility of Monetary Policy. *American Political Science Review* 97(3): 407–23.

Knack, Steven. 2000. Does Foreign Aid Promote Democracy? IRIS Center Working Paper 238. College Park: University of Maryland.

Kopstein, Jeffrey. 2003. Post-Communist Democracy: Legacies and Outcomes. *Comparative Politics* 35(2): 231–50.

Kopstein, Jeffrey. 2006. The Transatlantic Divide over Democracy Promotion. *The Washington Quarterly* 29(2): 85–98.

Krieckhaus, Jonathan. 2006. Democracy and Economic Growth: How Regional Context Influences Regime Effects. *British Journal of Political Science* 36: 317–40.

Lake, David, and Matthew Baum. 2001. The Invisible Hand of Democracy: Political Control and the Provision of Public Services. *Comparative Political Studies* 34(6): 587–621.

Lancaster, Carol. 2007. *Foreign Aid: Diplomacy, Development, Domestic Politics*. Chicago: University of Chicago Press.

Lancaster, Carol, and Ann Van Dusen. 2005. *Organizing U.S. Foreign Aid*. Washington, DC: Brookings Institution Press.

Landa, Dimitri, and Ethan B. Kapstein. 2001. Inequality, Growth and Democracy. *World Politics* 53(2): 264–96.

Larrabee, F. Stephen. 2006. Danger and Opportunity in Eastern Europe. *Foreign Affairs* 85(6): 117–31.

Lee, Junhan. 2002. Primary Causes of Asian Democratization: Dispelling Conventional Myths. *Asian Survey* 42(6): 821–37.

Lipset, Seymour Martin. 1959. Some Social Requisites of Democracy. *American Political Science Review* 53(1): 69–105.

Lopez-Cordova, J. Ernesto, and Christopher Meissner. 2005. The Globalization of Trade and Democracy, 1870–2000. NBER Working Paper 11117. Cambridge, MA: National Bureau of Economic Research.

Mandela, Nelson. 2002. *No Easy Walk to Freedom*. London: Penguin Classics.

Mansfield, Edward, and Jon C. Pevehouse. 2006. Democratization and International Organizations. *International Organization* 60(1): 137–67.

Maravall, Jose Maria. 1995. The Myth of the Authoritarian Advantage. *Economic Reform and Democracy*. Eds. Larry Diamond and Marc F. Plattner. Baltimore, MD: Johns Hopkins University Press.

Marshall, Monty G., and Keith Jaggers. 2005. *Polity IV Project: Political Regime Characteristics and Transactions, 1800–2002*. University of Maryland, www.cidcm.umd.edu/polity. Accessed on 15 September 2007.

Mello, Luiz, and Erwin R. Tiongson. 2006. Income Inequality and Redistributive Government Spending. *Public Finance Review* 34(3): 282–305.

Meltzer, Allan, and Scott Richard. 1981. A Rational Theory of the Size of Government. *Journal of Political Economy* 89(5): 914–27.

Milanovic, Branko. 2005. Relationship between Income and Democracy Re-examined, 1820–2000: A Non-Parametric Approach. Mimeo, World Bank.

Munck, Geraldo L., and Jay Verkuilen. 2002. Conceptualizing and Measuring Democracy: Evaluating Alternative Indices. *Comparative Political Studies* 35(1): 5–34.

Nelson, Joan M. 1995. Linkages between Politics and Economics. *Economic Reform and Democracy*. Eds. Larry Diamond and Marc F. Plattner. Baltimore, MD: Johns Hopkins University Press.

North, Douglass. 1990. *Institutions, Institutional Change, and Economic Performance*. New York: Cambridge University Press.

Olson, Mancur. 1965. *The Logic of Collective Action*. Cambridge, MA: Harvard University Press.

Olson, Mancur. 1982. *The Rise and Decline of Nations*. New Haven, CT: Yale University Press.

Papaioannou, Elias, and Gregorios Siourounis. 2004. Democratization and Growth. London Business School Working Paper. London: London Business School.

Persson, Torsten, and Guido Tabellini. 2003. *The Economic Effects of Constitutions*. Cambridge, MA: MIT Press.

Persson, Torsten, and Guido Tabellini. 2006. Democratic Capital: The Nexus of Political and Economic Change. NBER Working Paper 12175. Cambridge, MA: National Bureau of Economic Research.

Pevehouse, Jon C. 2002. Democracy from the Outside-In? International Organizations and Democratization. *International Organization* 56(3): 515–49.

Plümper, Thomas, and Martin, Christopher. 2004. Democracy, Government Spending, and Economic Growth: A Political-Economic Explanation of the Barro-Effect. *Public Choice* 117(1–2): 27–50.

Przeworski, Adam. 1991. *Democracy and the Market*. New York: Cambridge University Press.

Rabello de Castro, Roberto, and Marcio Ronci. 1991. Sixty Years of Populism in Brazil. *The Macroeconomics of Populism in Latin America*. Eds. Rudiger Dornbusch and Sebastian Edwards. Chicago: University of Chicago Press.

Radelet, Steven. 2003. *Challenging Foreign Aid: A Policymaker's Guide to the Millennium Challenge Account.* Washington, DC: Center for Global Development.

Rais, Rasul B. 1988. Pakistan in 1987: Transition to Democracy. *Asian Survey* 28(2): 126–36.

Ramey, G., and V.A. Ramey. 1995. Cross-Country Evidence on the Link between Volatility and Growth. *American Economic Review* 85: 1138–51.

Ramo, Joshua Cooper. 2004. *The Beijing Consensus.* London: The Foreign Policy Centre.

Rao, Vaman. 1984. Democracy and Economic Development. *Studies in Comparative International Development* 19(4): 67–81.

Remmer, Karen. 1993. Political Economy of Elections in Latin America. *American Political Science Review* 87: 393–407.

Rigobon, Roberto, and Dani Rodrik. 2004. Rule of Law, Democracy, Openness, and Income: Estimating the Interrelationships. NBER Working Paper 10750. Cambridge, MA: National Bureau of Economic Research.

Rivera-Batiz, Francisco L. 2002. Democracy, Governance, and Economic Growth: Theory and Evidence. *Review of Development Economics* 6(2): 225–47.

Rodrik, Dani. 1999. Where Did All the Growth Go? External Shocks, Social Conflict, and Growth Collapses. *Journal of Economic Growth* 4(4): 385–412.

Rodrik, Dani. 2000. Participatory Politics, Social Cooperation, and Economic Stability. *American Economic Review* 90(2): 140–44.

Rodrik, Dani, and Romain Wacziarg. 2005. Do Democratic Transitions Produce Bad Economic Outcomes? *American Economic Review* 95(2): 50–5.

Rose, Gideon. 2000/2001. Democracy Promotion and American Foreign Policy: A Review Essay. *International Security* 25(3): 186–203.

Rueda, David. 2001. Political Parties and Economic Policy in Industrialized Democracies: An Insider–Outsider Partisanship Model. Presented at the Conference on the Comparative Political Economy of Developed and Less Developed Countries. Yale University Center for International and Area Studies, May 4–5, 2001.

Russett, Bruce. 1964. Inequality and Instability: The Relation of Land Tenure to Politics. *World Politics* 16(3): 442–54.

Sachs, Jeffrey. 1989. Social Conflict and Populist Policies in Latin America. NBER Working Paper 2897. Cambridge, MA: National Bureau of Economic Research.

Satyanath, Shanker, and Arvind Subramanian. 2004. What Determines Long-Run Macroeconomic Stability? Democratic Institutions. IMF Working Paper 04/215. Washington, DC: International Monetary Fund.

Schuknecht, Ludger. 1996. Political Business Cycles and Fiscal Policies in Developing Countries. *Kyklos* 49: 155–70.

Sen, Amartya. 1994. *Poverty and Famines*. Oxford: Oxford University Press.

Sender, John. 1999. Africa's Economic Performance: Limitations of the Current Consensus. *Journal of Economic Perspectives* 13(3): 89–114.

Stewart, Frances. 2002. Horizontal Inequalities: A Neglected Dimension of Development. Queen Elizabeth House Working Paper 81. Oxford: Oxford University.

Svensson, Jakob. 1999. Aid, Growth and Democracy. *Economics and Politics* 11(3): 275–97.

Svolik, Milan. 2007. Authoritarian Reversals and Democratic Consolidation. Unpublished Working Paper, University of Illinois at Urbana-Champagne.

Tavares, José, and Romain Wacziarg. 2001. How Democracy Affects Growth. *European Economic Review* 45(8): 1341–79.

Tay, Simon S.C., and Yeo Lay Hwee. 2006. *Elections in Asia: Making Democracy Work*. Singapore: Marshall Cavendish.

Tilly, Charles. 2003. Inequality, Democratization and De-Democratization. *Sociological Theory* 21(1): 37–43.

Tilly, Charles. 2007. *Democracy*. New York: Cambridge University Press.

University of Texas Inequality Project (UTIP). 2006. *Estimated Household Income Inequality Data Set*. utip.gov.utexas.edu Accessed on 20 August 2006.

Van de Walle, Nicholas. 1999. *African Economies and the Politics of Permanent Crisis, 1979–1999*. New York: Cambridge University Press.

Wacziarg, Romain T., and Karen Horn Welch. 2003. Trade Liberalization and Growth: New Evidence. NBER Working Paper 10152. Cambridge, MA: National Bureau of Economic Research.

Wade, Robert. 1990. *Governing the Market: Economic Theory and the Role of Government in East Asian Industrialization*. Princeton, NJ: Princeton University Press.

Weyland, Kurt. 1998. Swallowing the Bitter Pill. *Comparative Political Studies* 31(5): 539–68.

Weyland, Kurt. 1999. Neoliberal Populism in Latin America and Eastern Europe. *Comparative Politics* 31(4): 379–401.

Weyland, Kurt. 2002. *The Politics of Market Reform in Fragile Democracies*. Princeton, NJ: Princeton University Press.

Weyland, Kurt. 2003. Neopopulism and Neoliberalism in Latin America: How Much Affinity? *Third World Quarterly* 24(6): 1095–115.

Williamson, John, and Stephan Haggard. 1994. The Political Conditions of Economic Reform. *The Political Economy of Policy Reform*. Ed. J. Williamson. Washington, DC: Institute for International Economics.

World Bank. 2005. *Economic Growth in the 1990s*. New York: Oxford University Press.

World Bank. 2006. *World Development Report*. New York: Oxford University Press.

World Bank Database of Political Institutions. 2005. www.worldbank.org.

World Development Indicators (WDI). 2006. www.worldbank.org/data/wdi2005.

Wright, Joseph. 2008. Political Competition and Democratic Stability in New Democracies. *British Journal of Political Science* 38: 221–45.

Yang, David. 2006. The Persisting Poverty of Strategic Analysis in U.S. Democracy Assistance Abroad. *Short of the Goal: U.S. Policy and Poorly Performing States*. Eds. Nancy Birdsall, Milan Vaishav, and Robert L. Ayres. Washington, DC: Center for Global Development.

INDEX